"Anthony DeStefano's new book is a powerful response to the 'new atheist' movement that is sweeping the globe. It will help people of all faiths to stand up to the aggressive attacks of these fervent unbelievers."

—CARDINAL RENATO MARTINO, PRESIDENT
EMERITUS OF THE PONTIFICAL COUNCIL
FOR JUSTICE AND PEACE AND FORMER
PERMANENT OBSERVER OF THE HOLY
SEE TO THE UNITED NATIONS

PRAISE FOR
INSIDE THE ATHEIST MIND

"Most atheists are pretty bitter, angry, and humorless souls. They will probably not like Anthony DeStefano's stinging and entirely hilarious takedown of the smug and arrogant brand of pseudo-intellectualism that modern atheism has become. As his targets whine DeStefano will shine, and his revealing book will enlighten, entertain, and probably melt some snowflakes!"

—MIKE HUCKABEE, FORMER
GOVERNOR OF ARKANSAS

"I'm thrilled that someone has finally decided to take atheism head on. I applaud DeStefano's dedication and carefully researched work. This book is funny, honest, raw, and will probably offend quite a few people, but I believe that everyone—no matter what beliefs they hold to—should take the time to dig in for themselves. You won't regret it."

—GLENN BECK, POLITICAL COMMENTATOR,
AUTHOR, AND MEDIA PERSONALITY

"*Inside the Atheist Mind* is a powerful retort to today's aggressive proponents of atheism, revealing how illogical and intellectually bankrupt their arguments truly are. Anthony DeStefano uses irony, sarcasm, and above all, an abundance of well-researched facts to debunk the philosophy of modern atheists—which is so often hollow and hypocritical. This book will help equip Christians and all people of faith to confidently defend themselves in the face of increasingly hostile attacks from unbelievers."

—RICK SANTORUM, FORMER US
SENATOR FROM PENNSYLVANIA

"Some children behave so very, very badly that reasoning with them is to cast one's pearls before swine. Anthony DeStefano understands this and happily spares not the rod in giving these wayward little beasties—known as the "new atheists"—the sound and proper hiding they so richly deserve. I brazenly defy anyone who thinks his atheism reasonable to read this wise and witty book."

—ERIC METAXAS, #1 *NEW YORK TIMES* BESTSELLING AUTHOR AND HOST OF THE NATIONALLY SYNDICATED ERIC METAXAS SHOW

"The superstition that is modern-day atheism is torn apart in this new, insightful book. Exposing these atheists for who they really are, Anthony DeStefano runs circles around their now debunked attempt to fool the public. You'll find this book empowering, revealing, and enlightening."

—JASON CHAFFETZ, FOX NEWS COMMENTATOR AND FORMER US CONGRESSMAN FROM UTAH

"In his previous books, Anthony DeStefano brought the wonders of faith, prayer, and Heaven to the masses. In this new book, he delivers a devastating look at the intolerance of the 'new atheists' who seek to drive any public expression of faith into the shadows and to make those who believe in God feel as though they are uneducated and naive lemmings. The book shows the critical role that faith and religion have played in the important fields of science, art, literature, and music, among others, despite the claims of the new atheists that religion is the enemy of progress."

—KEN BLACKWELL, SENIOR FELLOW FOR HUMAN RIGHTS AND CONSTITUTIONAL GOVERNANCE AT THE FAMILY RESEARCH COUNCIL, FORMER SECRETARY OF STATE AND STATE TREASURER OF OHIO, AND FORMER MAYOR OF CINCINNATI

Inside the
ATHEIST
MIND

Inside the
ATHEIST
MIND

UNMASKING THE RELIGION OF THOSE
WHO SAY THERE IS NO GOD

ANTHONY DeSTEFANO

NELSON
BOOKS

An Imprint of Thomas Nelson

Published in Nashville, Tennessee, by Nelson Books, an imprint of Thomas Nelson. Nelson Books and Thomas Nelson are registered trademarks of HarperCollins Christian Publishing, Inc.

Thomas Nelson titles may be purchased in bulk for educational, business, fund-raising, or sales promotional use. For information, please e-mail SpecialMarkets@ThomasNelson.com.

ISBN 978-0-7180-8056-3 (HC)
ISBN 978-0-7180-8059-4 (eBook)
ISBN 978-1-4002-0824-1 (TP)

Library of Congress Cataloging-in-Publication Data

Names: DeStefano, Anthony, author.
Title: Inside the atheist mind : unmasking the religion of those who say there is no God / Anthony DeStefano.
Description: Nashville : Thomas Nelson, 2018. | Includes bibliographical references.
Identifiers: LCCN 2017038905 | ISBN 9780718080563 (hardcover)
Subjects: LCSH: Atheism.
Classification: LCC BL2747.3 .D428 2018 | DDC 211/.8--dc23 LC record available at https://lccn.loc.gov/2017038905

Printed in the United States of America

19 20 21 22 23 LSC 10 9 8 7 6 5 4 3 2 1

This book is dedicated to
Father Frank Pavone

CONTENTS

A NOTE TO ATHEISTS

If you are a militant atheist—the kind who loves the writings of Christopher Hitchens, Richard Dawkins, Sam Harris, and that whole crop of arrogant unbelievers who are in such vogue today—please note that this book is not written for you. My purpose is not to convince you to believe in God or to prove God's existence in any way. There are hundreds of books on the market that do that already.

No, this book is not *for* you. It's *about* you. It's about all those wonderfully deceptive, malicious, ignorant, cowardly, and hateful things you say and do on a regular basis.

This book is also not meant for agnostics who are sincerely searching for the truth, or for people who are angry at God because of some terrible suffering they have endured. Again, there are many good resources that attempt to help people who are honestly struggling with their faith.

No, the focus of this book is on those obnoxious and aggressive "new atheists" who not only reject God but also wish to evangelize the whole world with their Gospel of Nothingness.

In the opinion of this writer, too many books written in response to these pseudo-intellectual blowhards have been altogether too nice. The authors have all tried to be kind and reasonable and amiable in an effort to demonstrate that believers don't have to sink into the mud in order to defend the faith. That tact is charitable and extremely admirable. But unfortunately, it just doesn't work with bullies. And that's exactly what modern-day atheists are—bullies.

So if you happen to be one of these militant atheists and you intend to read further, please don't expect the sort of kind and gentle approach you've experienced when dealing with believers. There won't be any coddling, respect for your views, friendly debate, dialogue, or turning the other cheek. Not in this book.

I'm afraid there is only one way to deal with bullies—even in this politically correct world—and that is to crush them.

CHAPTER 1

THE ARROGANCE OF THE ATHEISTS

I'm sure you've seen them before—arrogant, spoiled children. Kids who have no respect for their parents, their teachers, their elders, their peers. Kids who for some reason think they know everything, when in reality, they know nothing. They're condescending, obnoxious, prone to shouting, mean-spirited, and selfish. They're the kids who are always bragging that they have better clothes, better sneakers, better toys, better video games, better houses, better *everything* than their friends. They never seem to learn humility. They're always clamoring to be first. Always looking for attention. Always screaming to be recognized as the best. And if, by chance, they aren't given the credit they think they deserve, then woe to the guilty culprit whose fault it is—because that person will be treated to a noisy temper tantrum.

The type of arrogant children I'm talking about never take correction in a constructive way. They never take any kind of challenge to their "superiority." Their first reactions are always anger and petulance. Even worse, these children never seem to know when to keep their opinions to themselves. As someone once said of them: "Two-thirds of what they think on a topic is borrowed from their parents or older siblings, and the remaining one-third is based on whether they have an immediate desire for something."[1]

Now, kids like this usually have no basis for believing the things they do. Their attitude stems from some form of immaturity or insecurity. But if their arrogance, by chance, is founded in real circumstances—for example, if the child comes from a wealthy family or is "gifted" in some way—then their smugness is often of the very worst kind. Left unattended or uncorrected, these are the kids who become the notorious bullies and "haters" of the world.

But whether a child's arrogance is a consequence of wealth, upbringing, immaturity, insecurity, or simply natural disposition, the end result is always the same: rudeness and bad behavior. The end result is always a child who mistakenly thinks that everyone is beneath him; who deludes himself into believing that he is somehow smarter and better than everyone else, when, in fact, he is much worse.

Now, most of you who are reading these words have encountered children like this at one time or another. If you have, please fix that image in your minds for just a few minutes. It will be very valuable in understanding not only the subject of this chapter but also the theme of this entire book—because this image of the typical arrogant, condescending, bullying child that I've just described is, in actuality, the exact picture of the typical modern-day atheist.

That's right. Just as we've all seen spoiled, misbehaving children in action, we've also witnessed the spectacle of the new atheists spreading their particular brand of toxic arrogance throughout society. You know who they are. They're the ones who are offended by the slightest bit of religious imagery in public, the ones who are mortified if even a whisper of "Merry Christmas" escapes the lips of some well-meaning but naïve department store clerk during the holiday season, the ones who object vehemently to the phrase "In God We Trust" on money or the walls of government buildings. These are the self-righteous twits who cause a storm of protest whenever something overtly religious is spoken of in anything but hushed tones or behind closed doors. These folks are loud, nasty, unapologetic, and in your face. And, unfortunately, they're not going away.

In the following pages, I'm not going to focus on proving God's existence or showing how much sense it makes to be a believer. As noted earlier, plenty of books on popular theology do that already. Rather, my main purpose here will be to expose once and for all the blatant hypocrisy, dishonesty, and intellectual bankruptcy of the atheists themselves. For when you really look at what the new atheists are saying, you don't find a carefully constructed, logical argument against the theistic position; in fact, you don't find any argument at all. What you find is a lot of hot air. A lot of bluster. A lot of disdainful, unfounded, and empty dogmatism. Above all, what you find is arrogance.

Arrogance has been the calling card of atheists for a long time. It didn't start with Richard Dawkins or Bill Maher. Friedrich Nietzsche—the great patron saint of atheism, and, coincidentally, the favorite philosopher of Adolf Hitler (a fact atheists conveniently neglect to mention)—proclaimed famously in the nineteenth century that God was "dead" and "in his grave."[2] That preposterous pronouncement set the tone for atheistic arrogance over the next hundred years.

The militant atheists of the twenty-first century have raised this kind of pretentious egotism to an art form. Sam Harris superciliously writes, "It is time that we admitted that faith is nothing more than the license religious people give one another to keep believing when reasons fail," and that "atheism is not a philosophy; it is not even a view of the world; it is simply an admission of the obvious."[3]

Richard Dawkins haughtily states: "Faith is the great cop-out, the great excuse to evade the need to think and evaluate evidence. Faith is belief in spite of, even perhaps because of, the lack of evidence."[4]

Bill Maher rants: "Faith means making a virtue out of not thinking . . . and those who preach faith and enable and elevate it are our intellectual slaveholders, keeping mankind in a bondage to fantasy and nonsense that has spawned and justified so much lunacy."[5]

Christopher Hitchens condescendingly pontificates that "religion comes from the period of human prehistory where nobody . . . had the smallest idea what was going on. It comes from the bawling and fearful infancy of our species, and is a babyish attempt to meet our inescapable demand for knowledge (as well as for comfort, reassurance, and other infantile needs)."[6]

These are not arguments; they're snide, schoolyard taunts. And they demonstrate perfectly the deeply ingrained sense of superiority that modern-day atheists seem to have. By ridiculing believers for "failing to accept the obvious" and "copping out" and "evading evidence" and being "infantile," they show themselves to possess the very same traits that are so characteristic of the arrogant children I just described.

The position of the typical atheist today can be summed up in the following way:

Believing in God is not just wrong or misguided. It's tantamount to insanity. It's the same as believing in Santa Claus or the Easter Bunny. Since there is absolutely no empirical or scientific evidence for God, there can be no rational basis to believe in him. Since God can't be seen, felt, or heard with the senses, and since there isn't any geological or fossil record of him, and since he can't be proven mathematically, he simply *can't* exist. Period.

The reason why so many people throughout history have believed in God, they smugly assert, is because these poor ancient folk were ignorant of scientific facts. If they had known what we know, they *never* would have believed in something so absurd as God.

And as for the people today who still believe despite the marvels of scientific achievement, they've obviously been brainwashed by their religious upbringing, or have some kind of psychological *need* to believe in a supernatural being and an afterlife. They surmise this dependence comes from three primary sources: a fear of death, an unwillingness to accept the permanent loss of loved ones, and an inability to cope with life itself.

In other words, modern atheists think that those who believe in God fall into one of two general categories: we are either imbeciles or cowards!

This is not an exaggeration. This is *truly* what the new atheists believe. Read *God Is Not Great* by Hitchens, *The God Delusion* by Dawkins, or *The End of Faith* by Harris. The titles of these books betray the attitudes of the authors. Not one of these works presents a carefully reasoned argument against belief in God. They are all diatribes against *the very notion of belief.*

The bottom line is that atheists today do not acknowledge *any* connection between faith and reason. According to them, to be a believer means, *ipso facto*, that one must have below-average intelligence. It means that one has no ability to think rationally and lacks the necessary mental and emotional strength to face the problems of life unaided by recourse to prayer and other such "superstitious" practices. Mostly it means that one must be devoid of any real understanding of science.

The most laughable thing about this position isn't that it's unfair or untrue—which, of course, it is—but that it's so extraordinarily ironic. In fact, it's one of the most hilarious parodies of rational argument ever put forth by anyone, anywhere, at any time. Even the most cursory glance at history shows that the whole discipline of rational thinking on this planet—as well as almost all of our scientific knowledge—comes not from atheists, but from the minds of men and women who believed deeply in God.

Putting aside philosophy, logic, and mathematics for a moment, let's just take the field of science as an example and conduct an abbreviated survey of its principal historic figures.

First, who was the father of science and the father of scientific thought itself? The great Aristotle, of course. Now Aristotle, being an ancient Greek philosopher, didn't know anything about the founders of the world's major religions. But the man who organized and classified human thinking into categories such as biology, physics, zoology, and epistemology, and the man who is still recognized today as perhaps the greatest thinker who ever lived, did believe in divine intelligence. In fact, Aristotle rejected the notion of a strictly material universe and instead posited the existence of a first, uncaused cause.[7] This "first cause" of the universe is another way of saying "God." And Aristotle believed in him.

What about Francis Bacon, the father of empiricism? Empiricism is the theory that all knowledge is derived from sense experience—a position so dear to the hearts of atheists today. Bacon is also the person credited with establishing the inductive method of experimental science.[8] In other words he was the man who created the scientific method itself. Did he believe in God?

Yes, he did, and he was a devout Christian too. In fact, his last written words were in the form of a prayer: "Be merciful unto me, O Lord, for my Saviour's sake, and receive me into thy bosom."[9]

Pick another famous scientist from history at random—say, Leonardo da Vinci. Here was an inventor, a mathematician, a botanist, an astronomer, and an engineer. Da Vinci was the father of medical anatomy, paleontology, geology, ichnology, aircraft design, and a host of other scientific disciplines. He was the prototypical universal or "Renaissance" man. Did *he* believe in God?

You bet he did—and he created some of the most sublime religious paintings of all time.[10]

What about the father of physics: arguably the most prominent scientist of the Scientific Revolution of the seventeenth century, and the man who discovered the principle of gravity?

This was Isaac Newton—and he, too, believed in God.[11]

Indeed, the greatest geniuses of physics—including Daniel

Bernoulli, the man whose work underlies the operation of the modern automobile and the airplane wing; Wilhelm Röntgen, the discoverer of X-rays and the winner of the first Nobel Prize in physics; and Max Planck and Max Born, the founders of quantum theory and quantum mechanics—all believed in God.[12]

The supreme figures in astronomy—Copernicus, Galileo, and Kepler—all believed in God.[13]

The supreme figures in the field of botany—Brunfels, Turner, and Boerhaave—all believed in God.[14]

The father of modern chemistry, and the man who developed the first periodic table of elements and postulated the law of conservation of mass—Antoine Lavoisier—believed in God.[15]

The founders of electromagnetism—Volta, who invented the battery and whom the "volt" is named after; as well as Ampère, whom the "amp" is named after—believed in God.[16] Michael Faraday, who helped establish electromagnetic theory and electrolysis in the field of chemistry, believed in God too.[17]

Louis Pasteur, the famous French chemist and one of the main founders of bacteriology, renowned for his discoveries of the principles of vaccination, microbial fermentation, and pasteurization, and whose scientific work provided direct support for the germ theory of disease, was also an ardent believer in God.[18]

In medicine, Albrecht von Haller, the father of modern physiology, and William Harvey, the father of the modern study of anatomy, believed in God.[19] So did William Keen, the pioneer of brain surgery, and Joseph Murray, the Nobel Prize–winning pioneer of transplant surgery.[20]

Indeed the whole modern age of science was pioneered by believers. German scientist Wernher von Braun pioneered rocket technology. Ernest Walton was the first person in history to artificially split the atom. Wireless technology—including cell phones, radios, and our whole global telecommunication system—exists thanks to Guglielmo Marconi. Charles Babbage, the mathematician and analytical philosopher, is known today as the first computer scientist and the man who originated the idea of the programmable computer.

All of these men believed in God.[21]

And while we're on the subject of the pioneers of science, who do you think coined the term *scientist* in the first place? The answer is William Whewell, an Anglican priest and theologian, who also came up with the words *physicist, cathode, anode,* and many other commonly used scientific terms. Essentially, the very language used by scientists today comes from the brain of a believer.[22]

None of these giants in the field of science was an atheist. All believed in a Supreme Being who created and designed the universe. The list goes on and on and on. It includes scores of Nobel Prize laureates and presidents of scientific academies and institutions. It is a list that spans the globe and all of time itself. It is a truly staggering list.

And what do atheists make of that list?

Nothing! They ignore and dismiss it, as they ignore and dismiss so many other challenges to their thinking. Or they do their feeble best to explain it away. They'll say, for instance, that these God-fearing scientists didn't know about the theory of evolution or genetics or the big bang theory. They conclude, therefore, that the list really isn't as impressive as it may seem.

But even that objection betrays an ignorance of the history of science that borders on the insane.

When Charles Darwin wrote *The Origin of Species* in 1859—the work that first proposed the theory of evolution—he was definitely a believer in God. It's true that as he grew older, the spectacle of human suffering weighed heavily on his heart and caused him to doubt the existence of a personal Creator who cared about his creatures, but Darwin always struggled with his lack of faith. He was at times a Christian and at times an agnostic. But he never thought that his scientific theory was incompatible with the idea of God. Rather, he thought that while God did not have a direct hand in creating the different *species* of the world, he did indeed create the natural laws that governed the cosmos—including the laws of evolutionary development. Therefore Charles Darwin, the father of the theory of evolution, was *not* an atheist.[23]

And what of the science of genetics—the means through which evolution supposedly takes place? According to proponents of evolutionary theory, it is only through genetic mutation and the process of natural selection that life on this planet is able to undergo gradual development. Who, then, was the father of this field of study?

The answer is Gregor Mendel—an Augustinian friar and abbot of a Catholic monastery! This monk, botanist, and professor of philosophy was the man whose famous experiments on peas led to the formulation of the rules of heredity and to the proposal of the existence of invisible "genes"—which provide a basis for the science of modern genetics.

Well, then what about the big bang theory—the leading explanation of how our universe began? Surely an atheist must have had a hand in that.

No—wrong again! In fact, the man who proposed both

the theory of the expansion of the universe as well as the big bang theory of the origin of the universe—effectively changing the whole course of modern cosmology—was Father Georges Lemaître, a Belgian astronomer and Roman Catholic priest!

Yes, you heard that right. A priest came up with the big bang theory! If you don't believe it, look it up.

This cleric, who taught physics at the Catholic University of Leuven, delivered a famous lecture on his theories in 1933 that was attended by Albert Einstein in California. When Einstein heard Father Lemaître delineate his theory, he said: "This is the most beautiful and satisfactory explanation of creation to which I have ever listened."[24]

Now how could this be? How could the father of genetics be a monk and the father of the big bang theory be a priest? Didn't these men know what all modern atheists seem to take for granted—that the very theories they espoused contradict the idea of God and nullify the possibility of his existence? Didn't they know that their belief in God was therefore *absurd*? Were they really that blind?

Or is there, perhaps, another explanation? Could it be that these great men of science were not blind at all, but rather that modern atheists fail to understand the most simple principle of rational thought—namely, that explaining the scientific process of *how* the universe came to be does not in any way explain *why* it came to be. It does not explain the fundamental mystery of existence itself.

This mystery can *never* be explained by science. Even if the theory of evolution were true, for example, and life on this planet developed gradually over a period of millions of years, it would not in any way prove that God does not exist. Why?

Because, as someone once said, a slow miracle is just as much a miracle as a fast miracle.[25]

That's why Joel Primack, the American astrophysicist who codeveloped the "cold dark matter theory" (which seeks to explain the formation and structure of the universe) has written, "In the last few years astronomy has come together so that we're now able to tell a coherent story of how the universe began. This story does *not* contradict God, but instead enlarges the idea of God."[26]

You see, what atheists can't seem to understand (or probably just don't want to accept) is that no matter how wondrous the study of science can be, it is extraordinarily limited. Science will never be able to answer the question: "Where did everything come from?" or, "Why is there something instead of nothing?" or, "How can matter be eternal?" or, "Why is the universe so organized?" or, "How did life arise from lifelessness?"

The answers to these questions lie beyond the realm of science. That's why the greatest scientists in history have never been stone-cold atheists. Even Albert Einstein, who did not subscribe to the tenets of any religion, recoiled when people mistakenly thought that he might not believe in God:

"I am not an atheist!"[27] he stated emphatically. "In the view of such harmony in the cosmos which I, with my limited human mind, am able to recognize, there are yet people who say there is no God. But what really makes me angry is that they quote me for the support of such views."[28]

Einstein knew there was something more to the universe than he or anyone else could understand. In fact, he once said: "The most beautiful emotion we can experience is the mystical. It is the sower of all true art and science. He to whom this emotion is a stranger, who can no longer wonder and stand rapt in awe, is as good as dead."[29]

Atheists want us to dismiss the notion of the mystical. They want us to believe that the world is made up of physical objects and nothing else. They want us to believe that everything in life—our thoughts, our dreams, our passions, our loves, our hates, our hopes, our virtues, our sins, our griefs, our arts, our deepest desires for eternal life—that *all* of this is purely the result of biochemical reactions and the movement of subatomic particles!

That's not rational thinking. That's superstition!

Yet atheists continue to repeat their moronic mantra: "It's *absurd* to believe in God. It's *obvious* that he doesn't exist. It's *ridiculous* to have faith in something you can't see. All religious belief *contradicts* scientific and empirical evidence. Human beings only *invented* the concept of God because they want to go to heaven."

Amazing!

Bear in mind that we've only just scratched the surface. We've only talked about scientists in this chapter. We haven't even mentioned the greatest historians, painters, sculptors, architects, musicians, novelists, poets, generals, monarchs, explorers, and doctors. We just don't have the time or space to list the supreme figures in these fields. But if we did, rest assured that the overwhelming majority believed in God.

Once again, the point here is not to prove God's existence by providing an all-star list of believers. Nor is it to prove that any particular religion is correct. Nor is it even to disprove the atheist position. The point is simply to demonstrate the mind-boggling arrogance of modern-day atheists. These pompous prigs ridicule believers for being "infantile" and "unwilling to face facts," yet they dismiss not only the greatest figures of science but also the greatest minds in history—as well as the vast majority of people from all places and all time periods.

Which brings us back to the example of the arrogant, bullying children we began with. You can take children like that by the hand and patiently explain your thinking to them. You can show them a hundred examples of why their behavior is rude and condescending. You can try everything under the sun to be polite and argue reasonably with them. But none of it ever does any good. Common sense and appeals to logic just aren't effective against deeply ingrained, false pride.

What, then, is the remedy?

Well, some old-fashioned parents, completely out of vogue with modern methods of child-rearing, might suggest that in the worst cases of childish arrogance, a light spanking is in order. While this tactic might offend some of today's politically correct psychologists or sociologists, the fact is that sometimes this is the only thing that works.

And so, for the remainder of this book, we're going to do just that. We're going to give the new atheists the equivalent of an intellectual spanking. In fact, we're going to give them such a spanking that they'll probably cry foul and say we're being unfair and intolerant and hateful. They'll probably even throw a temper tantrum (they always do).

But that's okay. We're going to do it anyway. Not just because they deserve it but because they *need* it. That's the only way they're ever going to learn any humility. That's the only way they're ever going to grow up.

CHAPTER 2

THE IGNORANCE OF THE ATHEISTS

After arrogance, the predominant characteristic of the modern-day atheist is ignorance—tremendous ignorance.

In fact, atheists display more ignorance than perhaps any single group in the world. In truth it *should* be counted as their main distinguishing trait, and indeed it probably would if we were judging strictly according to the *volume* of information they seem oblivious to. But the qualitative nature of their arrogance—that is, the level of condescension they show toward believers—is so impressive that we're compelled to give ignorance second place, if only to be fair to them.

Now, *ignorance* is defined as a "lack of knowledge or information." It can take many forms, but the worst kind—the kind that can be really problematic—is that particular brand that carries with it some modicum of knowledge. Everyone has heard Alexander Pope's observation, "A little learning is a dangerous thing." That's exactly what I mean.

A small amount of information, gleaned from books or TV shows or college courses, can mislead people into thinking they are more expert than they really are. It can give them the *illusion* that they really have knowledge when they don't. And that illusion—just like mirages caused by hot air rising in the desert—can lead people to act in destructive ways.

In the early twentieth century, for instance, little was known about the chemical element radium. The dangers of radioactivity had not yet been discovered, so a few ignorant doctors began using radioactive materials as a therapy for various illnesses.[1] In fact, all kinds of products—including medicines, toothpastes, face creams, and even inhalers—were manufactured using these dangerous substances.[2] The result was a slew of new cancer-related deaths—all because some "experts" were in possession of a limited amount of knowledge.

This same dynamic can be seen in practically every area of life. How many young people have taken a few lessons in the martial arts and mistakenly concluded that they had expert fighting skills? What happens to these ignorant amateurs when they get into an altercation with someone who really has advanced skills in unarmed combat—or someone who has a weapon?

Or how about the world of business? How many people read a few books on entrepreneurship and come away thinking they have the business savvy of J. P. Morgan—only to waste their savings on some harebrained scheme that any seasoned business-person would have dismissed?

And what about all those cases of people who do a little medical research online and start to fancy themselves physicians, wildly misdiagnosing themselves and others based on a few random symptoms, consequently causing a tremendous amount of anxiety for everyone involved?

Or what about teachers who think they have great intellects just because they've managed to acquire a few letters after their names? How much havoc have these pedantic tyrants wreaked in the classroom? How much damage have they done to young, impressionable minds?

In all these instances and more, a small amount of knowledge leads to false pride, and then to faulty decision-making and disastrous judgments. That's why this particular brand of ignorance is so insidious: because it has the potential to be both stupid *and* dangerous.

And here again we arrive at the perfect picture of the modern-day atheist, whose ignorance of history is mixed with just the right amount of knowledge to be colossally misguided.

Atheists today are under the impression that belief in God has always been detrimental to civilization. In fact, they've asserted that, over the long course of history, those who have practiced religion—especially those who call themselves Christians—have been guilty of the greatest evils imaginable. They've repeated ad nauseam the tired refrain that "religion has been responsible for more wars, murders, and bloodshed than any other single factor"—and is therefore to be regarded as a blight on mankind.

Take, for example, some of the typical statements that have come out of the entertainment industry. Celebrities—most of whom are not exactly known for deep thinking—don't ever seem to hesitate to express their negative opinions of religion. Elton John, for instance, has said: "From my point of view I would ban religion completely. . . . The reality is that organised religion doesn't seem to work. It turns people into hateful lemmings and it's not really compassionate."[3]

Actress Gwyneth Paltrow agrees: "Religion is the cause of all the problems in the world. . . . It's what separates people. One religion just represents fragments, it causes war."[4]

Comedian Bill Murray declares: "Religion is the worst enemy of mankind. No single war in the history of humanity has killed as many people as religion has."[5]

And talk show host Bill Maher says: "Religion must die for mankind to live. . . . We are a nation that is unenlightened because of religion."[6]

This whole way of thinking is best summed up by Larry Flynt, publisher of *Hustler* magazine (and clearly a paragon of virtue), who said: "Religion has caused more harm than any other idea since the beginning of time. There's nothing good I can say about it."[7]

Nothing good can be said about it.
Religion is the worst enemy of mankind.
It should be banned.

Pretty powerful words. One would think they would be backed up by solid evidence, but alas, they are not. They never are.

These nitwitted celebrities can't ever seem to get beyond clichés. I would venture to guess that not one of the individuals previously quoted has the slightest clue how our civilization came to be or what historical forces contributed to the progression of modern society. Most of them simply parrot ideas they've heard or read, which happen to agree with their own feelings or their, shall we say, "lax" brands of morality. When they do attempt to use arguments to articulate their beliefs, they usually refer back to the same old anti-Christian books, such as Hitchens's *God Is Not Great* or Dawkins's *The God Delusion*.

These books—which can more accurately be called "hit pieces" on God—are neither original nor insightful, yet they masquerade as serious works of scholarship and are quoted as such by atheists all over the world. In *The God Delusion*, Dawkins states that if the Bible is true, then God is "a vindictive, blood-thirsty ethnic cleanser; a misogynistic, homophobic, racist, infanticidal, genocidal, filicidal, pestilential, megalomaniacal, sadomasochistic, capriciously malevolent bully."[8]

Armed with such a juvenile understanding of Scripture and such hateful adjectives to describe God, it's no wonder modern atheists view religion through a coal-black lens. It's no wonder their whole understanding of history is warped.

Briefly, atheists believe that religion—especially Christianity—has been harmful to mankind for five primary reasons: First, they claim that faith in God robs people of their ability to engage in critical thinking, as well as their ability to learn new facts that might contradict their superstitious dogma. Second, they think that religion is the enemy of art—that it is responsible for the widespread censorship of books, music, paintings, and speech. Third, they argue that religion teaches people to be helpless and rely on an imaginary Supreme Being, rather than on themselves—thereby destroying human freedom and enslaving mankind. Fourth, they say that belief in an afterlife stops people from making the most of *this* life. Fifth, they think that religion seeks power and encourages bloodshed, and is therefore responsible for countless deaths.

That's what atheists believe. But are any of these positions really true?

Let's start with the notion that religion is detrimental to critical thinking. As we discussed in the last chapter, many geniuses of science not only believed in God but also were ardent Christians. We saw how atheists choose to ignore this fact because it goes against their belief that science and faith are natural enemies. But if, for a moment, atheists actually tried to be fair-minded and asked themselves the simple question of why Christianity has produced so many great scientists, they might have realized the equally simple answer: because the Christian system of belief is founded on the idea that there *is* a rational God who is the source of rational truth.

Christianity teaches that there is a purpose and a design to the universe. Now, if something has a design, it follows that it must exhibit some kind of reasonable and rational behavior. It must, by definition, give rise to certain predictable laws and principles. This system of laws and principles is the whole basis for scientific investigation. That's why the practice of science, as an organized and sustained enterprise of the human race, arose in a civilization that was overwhelmingly Christian. One of Christianity's core beliefs is that *things make sense*, and furthermore, that it's our duty as human beings to find out how and why they make sense. That is the basis for all rational thinking.

Indeed it's impossible to study history without seeing the extraordinary role Christianity has played not only in the development of rational thinking but also in the *spreading* of such thinking—that is, the creation of an educational system. Though education was important in the pagan world, it didn't become institutionalized until Christianity began its march across the globe. The early Greeks and Romans had no public schools of higher learning.[9] It was Christians who established those.[10] When the Huns, Goths, Vandals, Visigoths, and other "barbarian" tribes overran what was left of the Roman Empire, it was the Christians who took the smashed European continent and imposed learning, order, and stability upon it. In the so-called Dark Ages, it was Christians again who painstakingly preserved, copied, and studied manuscripts from antiquity in order to pass them on to future generations.[11] Christianity, therefore, was responsible for the Renaissance, or "rebirth," of Greek and Roman culture.

Now, if the Christian religion had really been so opposed to critical thinking, why in the world would it have acted so decisively to protect and preserve the writings of Plato, Aristotle, and other pagan philosophers? Why wouldn't Christians have burned them in a big bonfire, as atheists claim they are so fond of doing to books that "contradict" the faith?

But there's more. It was the monastery system of the church that maintained the intellectual culture of the West for hundreds of years and gave birth to the first universities and libraries. These great institutions spread throughout Europe and provided a systematic—as well as integrated—form of public education for the masses. For the first time in history, individuals from all social and ethnic groups were included, without bias toward ethnicity or class. This contribution was revolutionary.

Nor was it just the Catholic Church that was responsible for the development of education. The Protestant reformers, who wanted everyone to be able to read the Bible, introduced to the world the concept of compulsory education for boys *and* girls.[12] This, again, was a radically new idea.

With all this focus on learning, is it any surprise that, later on, all but one of the first 123 colleges in colonial America were founded as Christian institutions—including Harvard, Princeton, and Yale?

And what of the criticism that religion is the enemy of art? Jack Huberman, in his book *The Quotable Atheist*, says: "Religious authority has always sought to . . . control and censor art and literature."[13] Likewise, Rob Boston writes in *Church and State* magazine: "The truth is, religiously based censorship [of the arts] by the government has a long history in Europe and the United States."[14]

Now, this is an area where atheists really have to work hard to maintain a state of ignorance. After all, how can anyone ignore the monumental influence that religious faith has exercised on *all* art forms—visual, musical, and literary? How can anyone say that religion has only been harmful to the world when the world's greatest paintings, sculptures, architectural structures, musical compositions, and literary masterpieces were inspired by, or directly commissioned and paid for by, religious institutions?

Is it possible atheists haven't heard of Michelangelo's *Pieta* or *David* or the ceiling of the Sistine Chapel, or Leonardo da Vinci's *The Last Supper*, or any of the religious works of Rembrandt, Bach, Mozart, Beethoven, Shakespeare, Dante, Dostoevsky, Milton, Dickens, and thousands of others? Is it possible they've seen the outside or inside of a Gothic cathedral or a Baroque basilica and not recognized the artistic heights to which a person is capable of soaring when inspired by religion?

The point here isn't that the creators of these magnificent works were Christian. It's that the creations themselves—infused with the spirit of religious fervor—could never have been conceived without the Christian faith. Just as scientific inquiry was founded on the idea that God and his creation are rational, so, too, was religious art founded on the idea that God and his creation are beautiful, and that humankind, being made in the image and likeness of God, has the power and the responsibility to make beautiful things too. This is the philosophy that lies behind so much of the world's greatest artistic expression.

And yet atheists continue to claim that religion has always been the enemy of art. Amazing!

They also contend that religion destroys freedom. But again, an unbiased look at history shows the exact opposite to be true. The biblical concept that all people are created in the "image and likeness of God" is the foundation of universal human rights—including freedom.[15] Before Christianity, human life on this planet was considered cheap. Infanticide was not only common but applauded. Newborn children were routinely abandoned on the hillside, left to starve or freeze to death.[16] Or they were killed outright through drowning—especially if they were baby girls.[17]

Adults didn't fare much better. Everyone has heard about Roman arenas like the Colosseum, in which whole families were bludgeoned to death, mauled by wild animals, or burned alive—just for sport.[18] The greatest and most respected ancient writers and philosophers didn't object in the slightest to these barbaric practices. It was Christians who finally banned them.

Why? Because the religious belief that all men are created equal is not a self-evident truth, as Thomas Jefferson famously wrote. To pre-Christian cultures, equality was a totally foreign concept. When the people of antiquity looked around at the world, they saw inequality everywhere—in physical appearance, mental capacity, moral conduct, economic and material possessions, and political power. The idea that all human beings were equal would have seemed preposterous to them.

It was the Christian religion, building on Jewish tradition before it, that introduced the bedrock principle that all human beings *are* equal—maybe not in physical traits or material possessions, but in dignity, in honor, in value, and in spirit. Most importantly, Christianity taught that human beings are equal because God created them and loves them equally and to an infinite degree.[19] Therefore, each human life has equal and infinite *value*.

This is a Christian insight—not a pagan, secular, or atheist idea. When people today proclaim that human beings have a universal right to express their opinions freely, to go wherever they choose, to buy and sell property, to live the way they want to live—they are expressing an idea that has a distinctively Christian origin. As Dinesh D'Souza says in *What's So Great About Christianity*:

> Christianity emphasizes the fact that we are moral agents. God has freely created us in His own image, and He has given us the power to take part in His sublime act of creation by being architects of our own lives. . . . John Stuart Mill's influential doctrine of liberty, which so many of us take for granted, is a direct inheritance from Christianity. It is no use responding that Mill was a product of the Enlightenment understanding of human freedom and equality. That notion was itself a product of Christianity. Where else do you think the Enlightenment thinkers got it?[20]

The point that atheists refuse to grasp is that Christianity espoused a revolutionary philosophy of equality that set into motion an intellectual process that gradually changed *everything*.

It was Christianity which rejected polygamy and adultery and exalted monogamous love—love geared toward the raising of children.[21] This is the basis for the traditional family, and no matter how much secularists decry that institution today, there is still no other force more stabilizing and beneficial to civilization.

It was Christianity that dramatically elevated the status of women at a time when practically every other culture in the world oppressed them. Indeed, the ancient world treated women like animals.[22] Read the Greek and Roman historians (such as Thucydides, Polybius, and Livy) to verify the truth of this! Women were the property of men, just barely higher than slaves. They had no rights at all. That's why they were so frequently exposed to the elements as infants. Christianity changed that.[23] Women had leadership roles in the early church.[24] They were supported financially when their husbands died. They were given an education. Instead of being abused, they were sheltered and protected. The whole medieval concept of chivalry arose because Christian civilization considered women to be of a *higher* dignity than men. The undisputable fact is that the women's rights movement of the last two hundred years has its roots not in pagan society, but in the principles of Christianity.

The same can be said about slavery. Atheists are always claiming that because Christians owned slaves at various times in history, the whole Christian religion is hypocritical. But that's nonsense. Slavery was practiced for centuries all over the world before Christianity came on the scene. No one ever criticized or opposed slavery in any systematic way—*until* Christianity.[25] From its very beginning, Christians discouraged the enslavement of fellow Christians.[26] And many early Christians purchased slaves for the sole purpose of setting them free. Because human dignity is at the heart of Christian doctrine, it was only a question of time before Christians began to realize that the very idea of "owning" another human being was contrary to their faith. By the Middle Ages, the institution of slavery—which provided the whole foundation for Greek, Roman, and Egyptian civilizations—was largely replaced by serfdom, a system which at least guaranteed basic human rights to all workers—such as the right to marry and to own property.

Later it was Christians who started the first antislavery movement in history. It wasn't Democrats who did that. It wasn't Republicans. It wasn't politicians or unions or any other kind of socially conscious group. And it *certainly* wasn't atheists. It was the church. Slavery came to an end in Europe mainly because of the work of Christian activists such as William Wilberforce, the famous British evangelical philanthropist.[27] And the successful antislavery movement in England—made up overwhelmingly of religious groups—took the lead in the international campaign to end slavery as well. By the early 1800s, two-thirds of the members of the American abolition society were Christian ministers.[28]

We see this same positive influence in *every* area of social reform.

Take economic freedom. The ancient world—built on the backs of slaves—had no real concept of the value of labor; yet Christianity—with its emphasis on human equality and dignity—revolutionized the workplace.[29] The concept of private property, property rights, workers' rights, and unionization all flow from the Judeo-Christian understanding of work and its proper relationship to social justice.

Take the world of politics. We've seen how the idea that all men are created equal has its origins in the Bible. Well, the whole idea of limited government comes from Judeo-Christian tradition too. The notion that there are certain God-given, unalienable, moral absolutes—such as the right to life, liberty, and the pursuit of happiness—that take precedence over any edict issued by a king, derives from Christianity. Is it any wonder that so many of the Founding Fathers of the United States, and at least fifty of the fifty-five signers of the US Constitution, were committed Christians?[30]

And what of the argument that Christianity is so concerned with getting people to heaven that it neglects to care for them here and now? This is perhaps the most preposterous of all the atheist claims. Before Christianity, there was virtually no institutional interest in helping the poor, the sick, the mentally ill, the disabled, the elderly, or the dying; but because of Christian teaching on the dignity of the human person, this societal callousness came to a screeching halt.

In the year 369, Saint Basil of Caesarea founded a three-hundred-bed hospital—the first large-scale hospital for the sick and disabled in the world.[31] Christian hospitals and hospices started springing up all over the European continent. These were civilization's first voluntary charitable institutions, and they were built and paid for by the church.

To this day, Christian influence permeates the health-care system. Just do an Internet search for Christian charities and see how many names appear. They are legion: missions to foreign countries, organizations to fight world hunger, inner-city soup kitchens, and ministries to assist those with every kind of infirmity. Think of the Red Cross and the Salvation Army. Think of Mother Teresa's Missionaries of Charity. Think of all the orders of nuns established to care for the diseased and dying. Think of all the Christian orphanages that have helped so many abandoned and destitute children over the centuries. Think of the thousands of religiously affiliated hospitals that are still in operation across the globe. There's simply no end to the number of charities founded in the name of Christ.

Why do they all exist?

The only plausible explanation is that, contrary to what so many feebleminded atheists believe, the Christian gospel is not just about getting people into heaven. It's about improving conditions in *this* life too.

And isn't that logical? If human beings are really made in the image and likeness of God, and if they truly have infinite value, then of course it's an obligation for us to be caring and compassionate—to help people everywhere, especially those who are least fortunate.

And yet atheists insist that Christians have their heads in the clouds and are happy to sit back and twiddle their thumbs as they await the Second Coming.

That's not an easy thing to do. It takes a lot of effort to keep your eyes clamped shut in the face of so many facts. How can anyone with even the most rudimentary knowledge of history be so ignorant of all these social, intellectual, scientific, cultural, political, educational, institutional, and artistic gifts that Christianity has bestowed on civilization? Christ said that a tree is known by its fruit. If the Christian religion is so terrible, how could its fruit be so bountiful and beneficial?

Bear in mind that we're not saying Christianity is perfect, or that it's been free of hypocrisy. It hasn't—not by a long shot. But in evaluating the cost-benefit ratio of anything, especially something as large as a religion, you must separate individual examples of evil from the overall pattern of good. You must look at the big picture.

And here again we return to that particular form of ignorance rooted in "a little" knowledge. Atheists love to go through history searching for "rotten fruit." When they discover some, they zealously rush to judgment without any real understanding of history itself. They find examples of Christians who've read the Bible simplemindedly, and they conclude that religion is the enemy of science. They find examples of Christians who banned certain books as blasphemous, and they conclude that religion is the enemy of education. They find examples of Christians who denounced various paintings as obscene, and they conclude that religion is the enemy of art. They find examples of Christians who owned slaves, and they conclude that religion is the enemy of freedom. They find examples of Christians who wrote about happiness in heaven, and they conclude that religion is the enemy of happiness on earth.

In a word, they look for dark specks on the vast canvas of history and, when they discover them, conclude that the canvas itself is completely black—when in reality, it is astonishingly white.

It makes you wonder if perhaps we're not just dealing with ignorance. Perhaps there's something else at work. Something deeper. After all, we still haven't addressed the fifth criticism of the atheists. We haven't talked about all the blood that's been shed in the name of religion. We haven't talked about the infamous Crusades or the dreaded Inquisition. Perhaps it's time we looked into those notorious events. In fact, while we're at it, maybe we should also conduct a brief survey of the blood that's been shed by *atheists* over the centuries.

It might be surprising to see what we find. In fact, it might reveal a clue as to why atheists seem so content to remain in a state of oblivion.

CHAPTER 3

THE RUTHLESSNESS
OF THE ATHEISTS

Have you ever heard of the "Big Lie"?

It's an expression that was first coined by Adolf Hitler in his 1925 book, *Mein Kampf*, and it was used to describe the propaganda technique that he successfully employed to catapult the Nazi Party into power, and then to maintain control of the German people for more than a decade. It's based on the idea that while small lies are easily exposed, refuted, and rejected, big, blatant lies can often seem more credible—if presented in the proper way. The reason is that good people have trouble believing anyone would even *attempt* to tell a lie that's enormous and obviously untrue. Therefore, if that lie is repeated often enough, and with sufficient conviction, the people who hear it will actually begin to question their own powers of judgment and start to believe what they instinctively know to be untrue.

It's a fascinating and evil concept, and it's worth listening to Hitler himself explain it:

> In the big lie there is always a certain force of credibility; because the broad masses of a nation are always more easily corrupted in the deeper strata of their emotional nature than consciously or voluntarily; and thus in the primitive simplicity of their minds they more readily fall victims to the big lie than the small lie, since they themselves often tell small lies in little matters but would be ashamed to resort to large-scale falsehoods. It would never come into their heads to fabricate colossal untruths, and they would not believe that others could have the impudence to distort the truth so infamously. Even though the facts which prove this to be so may be brought clearly to their minds, they will still doubt and waver and will continue to think that there may be some other explanation. For the grossly impudent lie always leaves traces [of believability] behind it . . . a fact which is known to all expert liars in this world and to all who conspire together in the art of lying. These people know only too well how to use falsehood for the basest purposes.

This technique of deception—though conceived by Hitler—was refined and put into practice on a massive scale by Joseph Goebbels, the Nazi minister of propaganda, who famously wrote:

> If you tell a lie big enough and keep repeating it, people will eventually come to believe it. The lie can be maintained only for such time as the State can shield the people from the

political, economic and/or military consequences of the lie.
It thus becomes vitally important for the State to use all of its
powers to repress dissent, for the truth is the mortal enemy of
the lie, and thus by extension, the truth is the greatest enemy
of the State.[1]

Thus, according to the main architects of the Big Lie, this
method of propaganda works best if the following three elements are in place:

1. A huge, colossal lie
2. Constant repetition of the lie to a mass audience
3. Suppression of the truth through a climate of fear

The most effective application of this technique, of course,
took place in the 1930s against the Jewish people. Goebbels,
making use of the mass media available at the time—including
radio, movies, billboards, and high-speed printing and distribution of magazines and newspapers—told the lie that the Jews
were subhuman; that they were evil incarnate; and that they
were responsible for all the economic hardships being experienced by the German people.

Obviously, this was absurd; but the Nazi propaganda
machine, working in tandem with the mass media, went into
full gear, repeating the lie in every possible way. They convinced
the German people that Jews were poisoning society and were
responsible for every evil imaginable, and that the only way
humanity could be saved was to rid itself of Jewish influence.

We all know what the "final solution" to this problem
entailed—the extermination of the Jews in the Holocaust. It

wasn't until the Allies crushed the Nazi army in 1945 and pictures of the concentration camps were shown to the German public that the Big Lie was finally exposed.

But while the forces of good triumphed in World War II, the Big Lie technique didn't disappear with the Nazis. It was utilized many times in the twentieth century with deadly results. And unfortunately, it is being used today in an effective manner by—you guessed it—our friends, the new atheists.

How so?

In the last chapter, we looked at the constant refrain that religion is responsible for more death, bloodshed, and war than any other single factor in history. That charge is shouted from the hilltops by atheists everywhere and then trumpeted by their sympathizers in the entertainment industry, the media, and the academic world. It's even familiar to schoolchildren, who are taught very early about the Crusades and the Inquisition and many other so-called crimes against humanity, perpetrated in the name of God.

We'll have something to say about those infamous events shortly, but the first point to make clear is this:

It's a lie. A big lie. A big, blatant, bald-faced lie.

Religion is *not* the cause of most of the wars that have taken place. It is *not* the cause of most of the murders that have taken place. It is *not* the cause of most of the bloodshed that has taken place. To even suggest such a ridiculous thing is to display an ignorance of history tantamount to imbecility.

The number one cause of war and bloodshed on this planet is, was, and always will be *economic gain*. One country or city or town wishes to take control of another's wealth and attempts to do so through force. Violent conflict ensues. People die. In ancient times the economic benefit might have been gold or silver or precious jewels or land or tools or livestock or slaves. In modern times the economic benefit usually takes the form of oil or technology or machinery or resources for manufacturing. No matter the specific object to be gained, the underlying motive is always the same—money.

Next to economics—and often connected with it—the most common cause of war and bloodshed in the world has been *territorial gain*. One country or city or town comes to the conclusion that it desperately needs more land—either for economic reasons (such as agriculture or oil), or because it wants more "living space" (such as the Nazi invasion of its neighboring countries), or the creation of buffer zones between enemies (such as in the Middle East or the Ukraine).

These are the two main reasons for violent conflict in human history—and nothing else. And they are *worldly* in nature, not religious. Beyond these, the principal kinds of wars have been *civil* or *revolutionary*. Within a given country, internal disagreement arises as to how the nation should be governed. Passions are enflamed, and war and carnage follow. Or, perhaps, a segment of the population revolts against its rulers for the purpose of changing the leadership or to gain self-determination.

Civil and revolutionary wars account for a vast number of bloody conflicts that have taken place on this planet, and almost all of them pertain to gaining political power. Very few have been about religion, faith, or God. In fact, even when the stated purpose of a war is ideological in nature, its *underlying* cause is usually civil, revolutionary, economic, or territorial.

For example, France and England have gone to war countless times over the centuries. But do you really think for one second that the reason is that the English are Protestant and the French are Catholic? Likewise, even though there was much talk during the American Revolution about fighting for the noble cause of "inalienable rights," is there any question that the main reason the colonists rebelled against Great Britain was to gain political and economic freedom? Even the Israeli-Palestinian conflict today cannot truly be said to be religious in nature. Yes, both parties make claims that God has given them a particular parcel of land. But the conflict is clearly a dispute over self-determination and the ownership of a specific geographical territory. The real rivalry—as any student of history or geopolitics knows—is *ethnic* rather than religious.

The point is that it is preposterous to claim that religion has caused most of the wars in history, when even a cursory glance at history shows otherwise. According to Phillips and Axelrod's three-volume *Encyclopedia of Wars*, which chronicles some 1,763 wars that were waged between 8000 BC and AD 2000, only 123 can be classified as religious in nature.[2] This represents 6.98 percent of all wars that have ever taken place. If you subtract Islamic wars from the equation, the percentage falls to a tiny 3.23 percent.

How on earth can atheists hysterically complain that Christians have caused so much bloodshed when they account for less than 4 percent of all of humanity's wars—while over 96 percent have been caused by other factors?

Bear in mind, we haven't even talked yet about the number of war *casualties*. If you look at a list of all the violent conflicts that have taken place in history—from the Vietnam War to World War II to the Chinese Civil War to the Mexican Revolution to the Napoleonic Wars to the Mongol conquests—you'll see that the overwhelming majority of people killed were the victims of *governments* and not religions. Rudolph Rummel, the renowned professor of political science who spent his entire career studying data on collective violence and war, coined the term *democide* to describe the all-pervading historical phenomenon of "murder by government." According to Rummel, in the last hundred years alone:

> Almost 170 million men, women, and children have been shot, beaten, tortured, knifed, burned, starved, frozen, crushed, or worked to death; buried alive, drowned, hung, bombed, or killed in any other of the myriad ways governments have inflicted death on unarmed, helpless citizens and foreigners. The dead could conceivably be nearly 360 million people. It is as though our species has been devastated by a modern Black Plague. And indeed it has, but a plague of Power, not germs.[3]

Ranked according to death toll, three of the ten bloodiest wars of all time were waged in the twentieth century: World War I, World War II, and the Second Sino-Japanese War. World War II alone, fought between 1939 and 1945, easily surpasses all other war death tolls, with upward of seventy million people killed.

Do atheists really need to be reminded that World War II had nothing to do with religion?

But it gets worse. The bloody figures we've mentioned only demonstrate the obvious fact that when it comes to war, worldly causes like economics and politics far outnumber religious ones. But what if we go deeper? What if we looked at *atheist* leaders and examined what happens when *they* are in power? What if we specifically looked at the wars and mass murders that have occurred during the reign of godless regimes, and see how they compared to "religious" wars?

And here we discover why atheists are always so content to remain oblivious to history. Here we see one of the main reasons for the Big Lie about war and religion. The truth is, atheist-based philosophies and leaders bear the blame for the vast majority of deaths caused by war and mass murder in the world. Just take a look at an abbreviated list of some infamous nonreligious dictatorships of the recent past:

Joseph Stalin (Soviet Union): 42,672,000 killed
Mao Zedong (China): 37,828,000 killed
Adolf Hitler (Germany): 20,946,000 killed
Chiang Kai-shek (China): 10,214,000 killed
Vladimir Lenin (Soviet Union): 4,017,000 killed
Hideki Tōjō (Japan): 3,990,000 killed
Pol Pot (Cambodia): 2,397,000 killed[4]

According to Stéphane Courtois in his book, *The Black Book of Communism*, atheist-communist governments killed more than one hundred million people in the twentieth century alone.[5] Ex-atheist Theodore Beale agrees: "There have been twenty-eight countries in world history that can be confirmed to have been ruled by regimes with avowed atheists at the helm . . . of whom more than half have engaged in democidal acts of the sort committed by Stalin and Mao. . . . The total body count for the ninety years between 1917 and 2007 is approximately 148 million dead at the bloody hands of fifty-two atheists."[6]

Let's just examine two of these dictators.

Joseph Stalin, who rose to power in the Soviet Union in 1927 and remained general secretary of the Communist government until his death in 1953, tops everyone's list of all-time murderers. Stalin was, of course, an avowed atheist. As dictator, he promoted atheism through the education system, antireligious propaganda, antireligious discrimination laws, the creation of a "League of Militant Atheists," and most importantly, a barbaric and bloody campaign of persecution against believers that he relentlessly pursued for twenty-five years.

Under his atheist regime, all religions in the Soviet Union—including the Roman Catholic Church, Eastern Catholic Church, Islam, and Judaism—were violently oppressed. Monks were killed, nuns were raped, and hundreds of churches, synagogues, mosques, monasteries, and temples were desecrated and burned to the ground.[7]

Stalin didn't limit his persecution to believers. He killed everyone who posed a threat to his power. During his dictatorship, he prosecuted a reign of terror unmatched in the annals of history—with mass executions, purges, and exiles to gulag labor camps.[8] He also methodically engineered famines on vast tracts of land in the Ukraine for the specific purpose of destroying the people there who sought independence from his rule. As a result, close to seven million peasants died in this farming area, once known as the "breadbasket of Europe."[9]

The total death toll under Stalin is difficult to estimate, but most historians put it between 40 and 60 million people.[10]

Now, let's look at Hitler. You'll sometimes hear atheists make the ludicrous claim that Hitler was a Christian, but that's just another lie. Hitler, as we've seen, was the inventor of the Big

Lie and a master of propaganda. During his early rise to power, he pandered to Christians in the same way he pandered to anyone he thought could help him achieve his objectives. Basically, Hitler wanted to *use* religion to enable him to gain power, to subvert it for political reasons, and then to eliminate it after his Third Reich had been firmly established. Indeed, once Hitler became chancellor of Germany, he began a brutal campaign of persecution of the church, imprisoning and killing large numbers of Catholic priests and bishops as well as Protestant leaders.[11]

Anyone who persists in the ridiculous belief that Hitler was Christian has only to read some of his private conversations, first published in 1953 by Farrar, Straus and Young. Here are some assorted quotes from the Führer:

- "The heaviest blow that ever struck humanity was the coming of Christianity. Bolshevism is Christianity's illegitimate child. Both are inventions of the Jew."[12]
- "National Socialism and religion cannot exist together."[13]
- "The reason why the ancient world was so pure, light and serene was that it knew nothing of the two great scourges: the pox and Christianity."[14]
- "Christianity is an invention of sick brains."[15]
- "Our epoch will certainly see the end of the disease of Christianity."[16]

As the Nuremberg documents clearly reveal, Adolf Hitler embraced the atheist tenets of fellow German Friedrich Nietzsche. It was the Nietzschean belief in the Superman (*Übermensch*), combined with a ruthless Darwinian view of social politics, that led Hitler to think he could create a German master race. Simply put, he believed that large populations could be genetically improved by the use of "selective breeding," which required the elimination of "inferior" races and blood strains in order to purify Germany's gene pool. Ultimately this delusion led to the extermination of approximately six million Jews and four million people from other religions deemed inferior by the Nazis.

When you add in all the other lives lost in World War II, the total figure comes to more than twenty million human beings killed as a direct result of this one atheist monster.

The historical evidence is clear: in the long catalog of human atrocities, atheism has produced a body count second to none. This is neither speculation nor biased opinion. It is incontrovertible fact.

"But what about the Crusades?" the atheists cry predictably. "What about the Inquisition?"

Atheists have been whining about the Crusades and the Inquisition for eight hundred years. Let's talk about those two events for a second.

The Crusades were a series of nine wars that took place between the years 1095 and 1272. The objective of these wars was to reclaim the Holy Land, which had been captured by Muslim forces several hundred years before. During the sack of the city of Jerusalem, Muslim armies had destroyed three hundred churches and monasteries and mercilessly persecuted the Christian population.[17] In the decades that followed, many other lands in Europe and Northern Africa fell to Islamic aggression. Finally, Pope Urban II called on Christians to act militarily. Basically, the Crusades were fought to take back something the Christians believed had been stolen from them.[18] They were born out of the violent aggression of militant Islam and were essentially *defensive* in nature.

Now, many wars in history have been defensive. When the United States declared "war" on terrorism in the early 2000s, it was responding to what it considered an unprovoked attack on the World Trade Center. The objective was not to seize Muslim lands, but rather to protect US citizens and their property. You may disagree with American policy and its motives, but the "war on terror" cannot be dismissed as a simple act of aggression against poor and innocent foreigners. Any thinking person would concede that it was more complicated than that.

The same thing can be said for the Crusades. Though atheists and anti-Christian historians love to condemn these wars as comprehensively evil, the truth is more complex. The Crusaders claimed to be fighting a war of self-defense against violent Muslim aggressors. They claimed to be fighting a just war. Nobody can be completely sure of a historical event's fine details, but considering the kind of Muslim aggression that still exists in the world today, why is that so hard to believe?

The Spanish Inquisition is also more complicated than atheists portray it. Two Catholic monarchs of the Renaissance—Ferdinand II and Isabella I—established the Inquisition as a court of law in order to identify and penalize a group of people known as *conversos*—Jews and Muslims who pretended to be Christian for political and social gain, but were secretly practicing their real religions.

Though it's undoubtedly true that innocent people were persecuted and killed during the Inquisition, certain mitigating factors must be kept in mind: First, the Inquisition began in the year 1478—more than five hundred years ago—when reliable records were not so easy to come by. Second, it was established as a state institution—*not* a religious one. Third, its severity has been greatly exaggerated by antireligious bigots whose real agenda is to use it as a stick for Catholic bashing.

According to Henry Kamen, author of *The Spanish Inquisition: A Historical Revision*, the common picture we have of the Inquisition as a quasi-Holocaust perpetrated by the church is unquestionably a myth; and the typical image of the all-powerful, torture-mad clerics behind it is largely an invention of certain nineteenth-century fundamentalist Christian authors who wanted to discredit the papacy.[19]

The actual number of people charged with crimes by the Spanish Inquisition was between 100 and 150,000. The actual number of people sentenced to death was only about 3,000.[20] Of these, none was executed by the church but only by the state. Moreover, these deaths took place over the course of *350 years*. Some historians contend that an additional 100,000 died in prisons due to malnutrition or illness—but there's no evidence for that. During this same period of time, the plague wiped out a third of Europe's population. There's just no way to accurately gauge the number of deaths caused by the Inquisition itself. Phony statistics abound.

The same holds true for the loss of life during the Crusades. An accurate count of the death toll simply doesn't exist. The common "guess" brings the body count to around one million total casualties in nine wars, stretched over a period of 177 years.[21]

These figures are tragic, to be sure—but they simply don't compare to the death tolls of the atheist regimes we just examined. Remember, atheist tyrants of the twentieth century murdered more than a hundred million innocent people! Yet atheists turn a blind eye to this recent and well-documented atrocity and instead persist in jabbering about events that took place eons ago under murky historical circumstances.

It's no wonder they resort to big lies. The truth is too damning for them to face.

But there's a deeper and more troubling question here. Why is it that atheists have been responsible for so many murders in history? Why is it that whenever an atheist regime takes the reins of power, life suddenly becomes cheap? After all, atheists claim that their philosophy is humane because it centers on humanity and not some make-believe God. But if that's true, why have atheist dictators tried to *destroy* so much of humanity?

The answer is something atheists don't want to hear. It's something they refuse to admit. And yet it's something so simple that even a child can understand.

The solution to this murderous mystery is that, without God, there is no final ethical judge of anyone's actions. Without God, there is no ultimate authority, no judgment day, no moral accountability. Atheist governments have killed more human beings than any religion in history because atheists don't believe in a God who says that killing is wrong. They don't believe in a "commandment" against killing. They don't believe in a commandment against *anything*.

Sure, atheists may think that certain crimes are reprehensible, but ultimately, their reasons are either emotional or practical in nature—not existential. In other words, they might believe it's wrong to commit a particular crime because they are personally repelled by it, or because they think society can't function properly in an environment of rampant criminal behavior—but not because the crime is wrong *in and of itself.* Not because the crime is an act which is contrary to the very nature of God—who *is* goodness and truth and life. Therefore, if an atheist dictator happens to believe it's not morally problematic to slaughter tens of millions of people—and he has the power to do it—why shouldn't he? (More about this point later.)

Beyond this, atheists don't believe in the infinite value of the human person. This is something we discussed briefly in the last chapter. Christians and Jews who are committed to their faith believe that human beings are created *in the image and likeness of God.* They believe that human beings have immortal souls. They believe that God loves each and every one of us—and that every one of us is therefore *worth more than the entire created universe.*

Atheists don't subscribe to this proposition. In fact, they think it's preposterous. That's why they create ethical systems based on savage philosophies like social Darwinism or Nazi Aryanism—and never on the bedrock principle that all human life is *sacred.* They just don't accept that principle as true.

Lacking this belief in the value and dignity of human life, atheist leaders are free to do whatever they want in order to seize power, maintain control, and restructure society according to whatever utopian vision of the future they happen to fancy— and that includes committing sadistic, merciless, cold-blooded acts of terror, and treating human beings as worthless garbage.

This might sound like a harsh judgment, but it's not. We've already seen how modern-day atheists are guilty of incredible arrogance, ignorance, and deception, especially when it comes to the blood-soaked legacy they've inherited. But we haven't even scratched the surface. We haven't yet described how atheists have attempted to implement the third element of the Big Lie propaganda technique. We haven't yet discussed how they've tried to suppress the truth about their ferocious philosophy through a climate of fear, intimidation, and intolerance.

But stay tuned. The worst is yet to come.

CHAPTER 4

THE INTOLERANCE OF THE ATHEISTS

How many times have we heard atheists moan and wail about religious intolerance? Next to all the "blood that's been shed in the name of God," this is surely their all-time favorite complaint. They love repeating ad nauseam the charge that people of one religion (usually Christians) harbor nothing but animosity and hatred toward people of other religions.

Meanwhile atheists, noble creatures that they are, sit back and shake their heads in despair, sadly contemplating the tragedy of hate in the world while they proclaim a doctrine that is—they assure us—infinitely more humane, loving, reasonable, respectful, and above all, "tolerant."

Yes, *intolerance* is such an important buzzword to atheists today. Simply defined, *intolerance* is an unwillingness to accept or endure views, beliefs, or behavior that differ from one's own, and an unwillingness to grant equal freedom of expression to others whose views, beliefs, or behavior differ from one's own.

Atheists claim to vehemently oppose any kind of intolerance—especially the loathsome brand practiced by men and women of faith. In rejecting a God-centered and "dogmatic" view of the universe, they embrace the philosophy of secular humanism, which considers reason, science, and social justice to be the highest ideals in life. Thus, atheists think that the hallmark of their own thinking is tolerance for other people and their varied points of view. After all, within a pluralistic society such as ours, there are bound to be many viewpoints that can be rationally arrived at, and in order for social justice to prevail, there *must* be tolerance and respect for everyone. Right?

But this is where things get a little confusing. Since the great majority of men and women has always believed in God, it should be obvious that religious faith must at least have *some* kind of rationale behind it. You might disagree with it—even passionately—but logic demands you at least admit this fact. On that basis alone—the testimony of vast populations of human beings spread across the globe and spanning all of time itself—one would presume atheists could muster just a little bit of tolerance (not to mention respect) for those who hold a religious point of view.

And yet, when we do a quick survey of comments from well-known atheists, we see something quite astonishing. Instead of carefully reasoned arguments filled with common sense, wisdom, understanding, justice, and "tolerance," we find the following:

> Our writings and actions are sincere attempts to rid the world of one of its greatest evils: religion.
>
> —*Jerry Coyne*[1]

If I could wave a magic wand and get rid of either rape or religion, I would not hesitate to get rid of religion.

—*Sam Harris*[2]

Some propositions are so dangerous that it may even be ethical to kill people for believing them.

—*Sam Harris*[3]

First of all, there are no great religions. They're all stupid and dangerous—and we should insult them.

—*Bill Maher*[4]

All faith claims are . . . equally rotten, false, dishonest, corrupt, humorless, and dangerous.

—*Christopher Hitchens*[5]

I think religion should be treated with ridicule, hatred, and contempt, and I claim that right.

—*Christopher Hitchens*[6]

Not much tolerance here, is there? Not much respect for other points of view. Not much of an attempt at understanding or analytical thinking. If religion is supposedly so intolerant, why don't we ever hear this kind of vitriol coming from the lips of the pope, or the archbishop of Canterbury, or the ecumenical patriarch of the Eastern Orthodox Church, or the top evangelical leaders in the United States, or the chief rabbi of Israel, or the Dalai Lama, or even most Muslim leaders?

Why are atheists the ones using such sweeping generalizations and such fanatical language? What could possibly account for this stunning lapse in secular humanist principle—this angry, misinformed, brutally intolerant, and blatantly hypocritical attack on all forms of religion?

Al Stefanelli, the Georgia State director of the organization American Atheists, reveals the truth: "Sometimes [intolerance] becomes quite necessary. Intolerance toward beliefs and doctrines that serve only to promote hatred, bigotry and discrimination should be lauded, as should extremist points of view toward the eradication of these beliefs and doctrines. . . . Many [people of faith] are sociopaths and quite a good number of them are psychopaths."[7]

Ah, now it makes sense. Intolerance must be eliminated at all costs—unless, of course, it is the atheist's intolerance toward people of faith. Then intolerance is not only acceptable but also necessary and praiseworthy, since it serves the higher purpose of improving the human condition. Moreover, believers are just psychopaths anyway, so who cares what they think or what we do to them?

Put another way: Atheists are tolerant—as long as you agree with them. If not, watch out! If you happen to come to a different conclusion than theirs about the existence of God (even if it agrees with what the bulk of humanity has always believed), you are nothing but a bigot and hatemonger and therefore *deserving* of discrimination.

We see this kind of "praiseworthy intolerance" on display in its most chilling and frightening form when atheists question the rights of parents to raise their own children in faith.

For instance, Richard Dawkins asks: "It's one thing to say people should be free to believe whatever they like, but should they be free to impose their beliefs on their children? Is there something to be said for society stepping in? What about bringing up children to believe manifest falsehoods?"[8]

Sam Harris agrees: "When we find reliable ways to make human beings more . . . genuinely enraptured by the fact of our appearance in the cosmos, we will have no need for divisive religious myths. Only then will the practice of raising our children to believe that they are Christian, Jewish, Muslim, or Hindu be broadly recognized as the ludicrous obscenity that it is."[9]

Psychologist and professor Nicholas Humphrey chimes in: "Children, I'll argue, have a human right not to have their minds crippled by exposure to other people's bad ideas—no matter who these other people are. . . . We should no more allow parents to teach their children to believe, for example, in the literal truth of the Bible."[10]

And Giovanni Santostasi, a neuroscientist at Northwestern University Feinberg School of Medicine, asserts: "Religion should remain a private endeavor for adults. . . . An appropriate analogy of religion is that it's kind of like porn—which means it's not something one would expose a child to."[11]

So religion is like porn. It's a ludicrous obscenity, a manifest falsehood. It cripples children, who must be protected from their parents by the state.

So much for tolerance.

Of course some atheists, such as author Zoltan Istvan, take a more "moderate" position. Writing in the *Huffington Post*, he says:

> I join in calling for regulation that restricts religious indoctrination of children until they reach, let's say, 16 years of age. Once a kid hits their mid-teens, let them have at it—if religion is something that interests them. 16-year-olds are

enthusiastic, curious, and able to rationally start exploring their world, with or without the guidance of parents. But before that, they are too impressionable to repeatedly be subjected to ideas that are faith-based, unproven, and historically wrought with danger. Forcing religion onto minors is essentially a form of child abuse, which scars their ability to reason and also limits their ability to consider the world in an unbiased manner.[12]

How considerate of Mr. Istvan! How magnanimous and generous to grant parents the legal right to expose their children to the religious point of view once they are past the point of impressionability! Believers should count themselves fortunate to have such a fair and thoughtful advocate!

No, I'm afraid the truth is clear. According to atheists, religious faith is much too "dangerous" to be taught to children. Despite the fact that it has sustained humanity from time immemorial and given rise to art, literature, music, philosophy, education, science, and humanitarian aid, it is really just a form of child abuse.

Now, some atheists today do think their fellow non-believers have gone a bit too far, but these sensible atheists are difficult to find. In fact, if you search the Web, you'll see hundreds of atheist-run sites under headings such as: "Christians are disgusting," "All religion is evil," "Is there such a thing as an intelligent believer?" and "Religion must be destroyed!" Look for yourself—it is a veritable online orgy of rage.

Yet amid the oceans of venom, amid the calls for religion to be mocked, outlawed, and banned, there are a few quiet voices of sanity that seem to represent a less militant form of atheism. These folks disavow the anti-Christian, anti-Muslim, and anti-Semitic rhetoric of firebrands like Dawkins, Harris, and Hitchens, and they try to give credit to religion for the contribution it has made to the history of humankind on this planet.

Though their efforts are greatly appreciated by people of faith, the truth is, these "kinder, gentler" atheists are actually very naïve. They don't understand the raison d'être of their own movement. They haven't thought through the atheist position to its logical conclusion. In their desire to be amiable, they've neglected to be accurate. In fact, they've missed the historical picture completely. If they truly realized how out of touch they were with their own long tradition of intolerant hostility and violence, they would never be so foolish to think they could change the boorish ways of their atheist brethren. That's just not going to happen.

You see, the climate of anger and fear that atheists have created today through their vicious and despicable attacks on religion is nothing new. It's been their modus operandi for hundreds and even thousands of years. It was present at the very birth of Christianity. Remember that Jesus of Nazareth—a humble Jewish carpenter who never once held a weapon in his hands—didn't die a natural death. He was brutally executed. He was a victim of his pagan state's intolerance toward his statements of faith.

Yes, the paganism of Christ's time was not exactly the same thing as the atheism of modern times, but they resemble each other much more closely than atheists would have us believe. The deities or gods of the ancient pagans were not at all like the God of Judaism or Christianity. They were purely mythological in nature—part of a storytelling tradition rather than a serious belief system. They were poetical rather than theological. Indeed, the pagans of Christ's time were morally ambivalent and decadent, just like the atheists today. They had no belief in a personal God who created the universe, just like the atheists today. They were pantheistic and nature-worshipping, just like the atheists today. Most important, their intolerance toward religions—especially Christianity—was of the same ferocious kind as that of atheists today.

The true ancestors of the Christian-bashing atheists of modern times are none other than the Christian-bashing pagans of antiquity. To understand the bewildering hostility atheists display toward religion today, we must view it through the lens of history—starting with the first Christians who were persecuted so savagely at the hands of the Roman state.

For hundreds of years after Jesus of Nazareth died, Christian practices were banned, Christian clergy were imprisoned, and tens of thousands of Christian families were mercilessly murdered in arenas like the Colosseum. Writing in the year AD 64, the Roman historian Tacitus described how the pagan Roman government treated the first Christians:

> Nero falsely accused and executed with the most exquisite punishments those people called *Christians*, who were infamous for their abominations. The originator of the name, Christ, was executed as a criminal by the procurator Pontius Pilate during the reign of Tiberius; and though repressed, this destructive superstition erupted again, not only through Judea, which was the origin of this evil, but also through the city of Rome. . . . Therefore, first those were seized who admitted their faith, and then, using the information they

provided, a vast multitude were convicted . . . for hatred of the human race. And perishing they were additionally made into sports: they were killed by dogs by having the hides of beasts attached to them, or they were nailed to crosses or set aflame, and, when the daylight passed away, they were used as nighttime lamps. . . . Even though they were clearly guilty . . . people began to pity these sufferers.[13]

Though the writer of this account was sympathetic to the suffering of the Christians, his language demonstrates that he, being a pagan himself, clearly believed Christians were evil and guilty of abominations, including "hatred of mankind." Indeed, it's eerie how little the tone of anti-Christian rhetoric has changed in two thousand years.

G. K. Chesterton put it best. Describing those first Christian martyrs—those poor men, women, children, and infants—all huddled together in the arena, quietly and courageously waiting for the ravenous lions to be released, he said: "There shone on them in that dark hour a light that has never been darkened; a white fire clinging to that group like an unearthly phosphorescence, blazing its track through the twilights of history . . . [a lightning] by which its own enemies have made it more illustrious and its own critics have made it more inexplicable: the halo of hatred around the Church of God."[14]

The halo of hatred. That describes it perfectly—a raging, intolerant, and inexplicable hatred directed toward people of faith everywhere; a hatred that is always completely out of proportion to their supposed crimes.

This hatred seemed to fade somewhat during those centuries when religious belief was more fervent, and when religions themselves held more power in the state. But it never truly disappeared. It was only hiding, waiting for a chance to rear its menacing head again the moment atheists began to acquire real political power.

And acquire power they did. During the French Revolution, antireligious crusaders such as Jacques Hébert and Jacques-Claude Bernard sought to begin a new persecution of religion as they attempted to completely de-Christianize France and establish a government whose official ideology was the "Cult of Reason."[15]

To accomplish this goal, French radicals encouraged the destruction and desecration of churches and cathedrals for the purpose of transforming them into "Temples of Reason."[16] The so-called Reign of Terror, which began in 1793, was marked by mass executions of "enemies of the revolution"—including Christians. The Catholic Church had opposed the revolution, which had sought to turn the clergy into employees of the state and required them to take an oath of loyalty to the new French government.[17] This new government, atheistic in the extreme, persecuted and executed thousands of believers. The death toll is estimated at forty thousand, with sixteen thousand killed by guillotine, and another twenty-five thousand in summary executions across France.[18] As many as three hundred thousand French men and women were arrested during a ten-month period between September 1793 and July 1794.[19]

Besides the guillotine, the atheist leaders of the French Revolution utilized other methods of execution, including the notorious practice of "republican marriages," which involved stripping couples naked, tying them together to a log, and then drowning them.[20]

It's important to understand that the perpetrators of these heinous crimes were not unintelligent street rabble. They were journalists. They were politicians. They were educated ideologues whose thinking was characterized by a philosophy of militant atheism.

This same philosophy was espoused by men like Auguste Comte, Ludwig Feuerbach, Karl Marx, and Friedrich Nietzsche. Not only did these atheists publicly denounce belief in God, but also they shared a white-hot hatred of religion and argued forcefully that it was humanity's solemn duty to destroy religious conviction altogether. To oppose this destruction, they claimed, was an act contrary to reason and historical progress. Tolerance was not part of their vocabulary.

It was these atheist philosophers of the nineteenth century who laid the ideological foundation for the atheist political leaders of the twentieth century. Their intolerance for religion and religious principles set the stage for the bloodiest wars and mass murders ever to take place on the stage of human history.

Remember what we discussed in the last chapter: Atheist regimes of the twentieth century—which included the Soviet Union under Lenin and Stalin, China under Mao Zedong, Albania under Enver Hoxha, and Cambodia under the Khmer Rouge—ruthlessly murdered more than one hundred million people. *One hundred million!* Don't pass over that figure quickly. Look at it. Think about it. Mull it over. One hundred million people wiped out—all forms of religion brutally suppressed, churches and synagogues desecrated and destroyed—all by militant atheists.

What was the reason for this carnage? The Christians and Jews who were slaughtered didn't commit any crimes. They weren't plotting revolutions. They weren't trying to amass political power. They weren't attempting to overthrow dictators. Their only offense was practicing their religion. They believed their first allegiance belonged to God—not the state. That was why the atheists who controlled the state butchered them. Indeed that's what always happens when atheists control the state. Whether it was the decadent emperors of pagan Rome, or the French followers of the Cult of Reason, or the godless dictators of the twentieth century, militant atheists showed their tolerance for people with other points of view by murdering them.

And that's why any effort to promote a tolerant atheism today is futile. Tolerance is part of the Big Lie. It doesn't exist. The atheist statements we cited earlier about the obligation of the state to restrict the rights of parents to raise their own children are the tip of the iceberg. As atheists gain more political power and exercise more control over media, academia, and the entertainment industry, their attacks on religious freedom always grow more blatant and egregious. It's part of who they are.

Indeed, a modern-day persecution of religion by atheists has already begun, and the evidence is all around us.

For the last fifty years in America, religious symbols, imagery, and sentiment have been systematically purged from the public square. Any kind of prayer—even nondenominational and silent prayer—has been forbidden in public schools. Quotations from Scripture—even the Ten Commandments—have been removed from courts and federal buildings. Government employees are no longer permitted to express themselves by hanging religious signs in their workspaces, but they are completely free to hang any other kind of non-work related, secular signs. Postage stamps commemorating religious holidays and holy people are hardly ever issued, while there seems to be no end to the number of commemorative stamps featuring secular celebrities like Janis Joplin, Jimi Hendrix, Elvis, Wilt Chamberlain, and Batman. Schoolchildren no longer have Christmas and Easter vacations, but rather winter and spring breaks. During the holiday season, religious images like crèches and menorahs have been eradicated from most public places, and those attempting to retain them can be sued by organizations like the ACLU and the FFRF (Freedom from Religion Foundation). Even reference to the word *Christmas* has been increasingly censored by advertisers, retailers, schools, and government offices. And while some secular aspects of Christmas (such as lighted decorations) have been retained to spur retail spending, they're usually showcased only on the condition that they be associated with an unspecified holiday season rather than the birth of Christ.

At the same time that this purge has taken place, atheists have mounted a relentless public relations campaign to mock the Christian faith—especially during Christmas and Easter seasons. Billboards paid for by groups such as the American Atheists have appeared all over the United States—including the Bible Belt—with confrontational slogans such as: "Who needs Christ during Christmas? Nobody!" and "Christianity: Sadistic God, Useless Savior," and "Grow up! You're too old for fairy tales," and "You know it's a myth: This season, celebrate reason."[21]

Such in-your-face advertising is obviously calculated to provoke anger and to ridicule people's deepest beliefs at the holiest times of year. If multiculturalism is such a sacred value of secular society, where are all the calls for sensitivity to Christian culture? Just imagine if similar billboards were posted against other religious faiths, ethnic minorities, or even popular secular beliefs. They would be declared hate crimes, wouldn't they? And yet, in twenty-first-century secular America, attacks on Christian beliefs go unchallenged.

How could this be? A recent Rasmussen poll reported that 76 percent of Americans still believe that religious symbols should be allowed on public land, and 83 percent believe that public schools should celebrate religious holidays in some way.[22] If this is the case, how could America allow itself to become a nation where all religious prayers, pageants, and holy days have been suppressed, while antireligious bigotry is not only tolerated but accepted as normal?

The simple reason is that many Americans have been taken in by the Big Lie. They've been hoodwinked into accepting that religion is somehow dangerous to the republic and that there must be an impenetrable wall erected between it and the government. If people dare to challenge this nonsense, they're shouted down and intimidated by a loud, rude, and unrelenting chorus of hisses from a hostile atheist minority.

The truth is, the Constitution of the United States says nothing about a wall of separation between church and state. When the First Amendment was ratified in 1791, it contained the Establishment Clause, which prohibited the government from establishing any state religion; but there's a huge difference between *establishing* a state religion and totally *excluding* religion from the state.

The framers of our Constitution didn't want the federal government to set up some form of church or interfere with the free exercise of religion. That was their purpose, and nothing more. The idea that the placement of Christian, Jewish, or Muslim religious symbols on public property is somehow a violation of the Establishment Clause is ludicrous—and the founders of this country would have considered it an obscene distortion of their intent. Indeed, Thomas Jefferson once said: "The legitimate powers of government extend to such acts only as are injurious to others. But it does me no injury for my neighbor to say there are twenty gods, or no god."[23]

For the last fifty years, unelected, secular judges in this country have routinely abused their powers with impunity. Not only have they restricted the religious activities of the government, but they've also restricted the free religious expression of the people. In his book, *Men in Black: How the Supreme Court Is Destroying America*, radio host Mark Levin states:

> The intensive and concerted effort to exclude references to religion or God from public places is an attack on our founding principles. It's an attempt to bolster a growing reliance on the government—especially the judiciary—as the source of our rights. But if our rights are not unalienable, if they don't come from a source higher than ourselves, then they're malleable at the will of the state. This is a prescription for tyranny.[24]

Tyranny—that is exactly what the militant atheist minority is always seeking to impose. No one with any common sense really minds when people say "Merry Christmas" in a post office or a government building. No one really feels discriminated against when they see a Christmas tree or a manger scene or a menorah in a public square. There needs to be a state of tyranny in place for such simple expressions of piety to be suppressed.

And that's just the kind of state we're living in today.

It's time to face facts. Atheists have nothing less than a totalitarian intolerance for believers. They are determined to root out and remove any remaining vestiges of Christianity from Europe and America, and even to deny parents the right to raise their own children with religious faith. They use the same language and harbor the same ambitions as the Communist regimes of the twentieth century. Though they've stopped short of employing physical violence to establish their vision of a godless utopia (give them time), they've instead driven their opponents from the public square with a lethal mixture of scorn, smears, deception, and legal intimidation.

But why? What could possibly account for all this fury? What lies at the bottom of this black and fiery hatred of religion?

Before we can answer that question, we need to lay a bit more groundwork. We need to enter into the atheist consciousness and actually try to understand the atheist mind. When we do that, we discover two striking qualities that have the potential to shed light on the deeper, more sinister mystery of the atheist's raging intolerance.

These two character traits—next on our list to discuss—are a profound moral cowardice and an astonishing lack of intelligence.

CHAPTER 5

THE SHALLOWNESS OF
THE ATHEISTS

We said at the beginning of this book that the most prominent character trait of modern atheists is arrogance, followed closely by ignorance. Indeed, these two qualities seem to be racing against each other, with arrogance always managing to win in a photo finish. If, however, we asked the question, "Which atheist character trait deserves the *longest* discussion?" there would be no contest at all. For, while any chapter in this book might serve as the basis for a book of its own, the subject we're going to deal with now deserves a whole shelf of books. In fact, there are so many examples of this particular atheist characteristic that it has been a herculean task to cut this chapter down to a manageable size.

Of course, the trait I'm referring to is *intellectual shallowness*. The fact is, there are only so many ignorant taunts that can be made by atheist celebrities. There are only so many arrogant lies that can be told by atheist authors. There are only so many ruthless murders that can be committed by atheist dictators. But there is simply no end to the number of idiotic statements that can come out of atheist mouths.

I really don't mean to be facetious here. The famed attorney Vincent Bugliosi (who prosecuted Charles Manson) was one of the most successful trial lawyers of all time, and even though he was an agnostic, he painstakingly analyzed the works of the three most influential new atheists—Richard Dawkins, Sam Harris, and Christopher Hitchens. After finishing his research, he came to the conclusion that *all* of their arguments were empty, illogical, and embarrassingly superficial.

In his book *Divinity of Doubt*, he said:

> In my various investigations throughout my career, I have found [that] . . . if you start out with a valid premise (not an ultimate conclusion), virtually everything you discover thereafter falls into place. . . . In this case, because the core belief of these three atheist authors was so intrinsically unsound . . . they could not present any solid evidence or even make any persuasive arguments . . . for the proposition that there is no God.[1]

"Atheism," he determined, "is really nothing but a sorry litany of non-sequiturs."[2]

Now, *non-sequitur* is a Latin phrase that means "does not follow." The dictionary defines it as an invalid argument in which the conclusion does not logically follow from the statements or premises that come before it. For example:

John Smith does not own a car. Therefore John Smith is poor.

Anyone with even the slightest modicum of intelligence can see that such a statement makes no sense. It may be true that John Smith is poor, but that fact cannot be proven just because he doesn't own a car. Perhaps John leases a car. Perhaps John is only ten years old and too young to buy a car. Perhaps he lives in the city and takes public transportation everywhere and doesn't need a car. Perhaps he is actually very rich and able to hire a limousine and driver. Perhaps he is rich but is in prison for tax evasion. Perhaps he has a phobia about driving.

There are many legitimate reasons why this individual named John might not possess an automobile; and yet, there are some silly people out there who would presume that John *must* be poor. To them, a lack of funds is the only possible explanation for his situation.

What can you say about such people? Is it really cruel to conclude that they are shallow or superficial or stupid? And here again, we come to the perfect picture of modern-day atheists.

Their reasoning—if you can call it that—is made up almost exclusively of logical fallacies such as the non-sequitur. They write books full of scathing attacks on God and religion that in the end prove absolutely nothing because their arguments are the most flimsy and shallow kind imaginable.

And the flimsiest and shallowest of them all is something called the "straw man" argument.

The straw man argument is a technique wherein someone oversimplifies, overstates, or misrepresents his opponent's position so it is more easily refuted. He basically creates a phony straw man for the sole purpose of knocking it down and claiming victory.

Atheists love this type of argument and use it all the time.

For instance, they are always making the claim that the Bible disproves the existence of God. They say: "If the Bible is really a true book (as you Christians believe), then God obviously doesn't exist because the Bible is full of lies, errors, and contradictions."

In other words, they first misrepresent the Bible by over-generalizing it (saying it is simply "true"); then they discredit this straw man misrepresentation; and finally they conclude they have refuted God himself.

Voilà!

Only that doesn't work. It's a completely false line of thinking. Not only is it illogical and invalid, but it's also extraordinarily shallow—not to mention intellectually dishonest.

First of all, even if you could prove that the Bible was full of errors, doing so would not prove that God doesn't exist. Millions of people all over the world believe in God but don't accept the Bible as true. Disproving the Bible might call into question some aspects of certain religions, but it would not call into question the existence of God. The two propositions—the Bible's accuracy and the reality of God—are not logically connected. To attack the Bible, as so many atheists do in order to bolster their case against God, is simply a non-sequitur. It's like saying: John Smith doesn't own a car. Therefore John Smith is poor.

Besides being illogical, the atheists' criticism of the Bible is profoundly superficial in other ways. For example, they make no distinction between literal truth and metaphoric truth. They frequently cite certain passages in Scripture that seem far-fetched to them—such as the story of Jonah being swallowed by the big fish—and then unleash a fury of ridicule: "This is just too preposterous for words!" they laugh. "How could a whale or fish swallow a man whole? How could a man survive in a whale's stomach for three days? It's scientifically impossible. He would have been digested. The story is obviously a myth on the same level as the tooth fairy. Therefore the Bible is false, and anyone who believes it is a lunatic." And so on.

Now for goodness' sake, how shallow is this line of thinking? It makes at least two invalid assumptions: one, that supernatural events are simply impossible; and two, that the story of Jonah must be taken literally.

In the first instance, the assumption that this event couldn't take place is not something that can be proven empirically. It's not even logical. After all, if God exists, why shouldn't he be able to suspend the natural laws? He created those laws in the first place! To simply assume that he can't is an example of circular reasoning: this particular miraculous event didn't happen because miracles, themselves, don't happen.

The second assumption is that the book of Jonah must be read literally—but that is *not* how all Christians and Jews approach this story or how they approach the Bible generally.

Though some Christians do adhere to a strictly literal interpretation of even this Bible text (on the grounds cited above—that God can perform any kind of supernatural miracle he wishes), most Christians take a much wider and deeper view of Scripture.

Christian doctrine holds that the Bible is not just one book, but a *collection* of books, written at different times in history and in different literary styles. It's true that the author of all Scripture is God, but God used many different people as instruments to write down his words over the course of the centuries, and those people employed many different literary techniques. As Bishop Robert Barron has said so well in his popular YouTube videos, the Bible is more like a *library* than one single book.[3]

Now, if you walk into a library and ask a librarian, "Should I take everything in this building literally?" you won't receive a blanket yes-or-no answer. The librarian would be more nuanced and say something like: "Well, there are many sections in this library. If you go over to the science or history departments, then you will certainly find that they are filled with historic facts. However, if you go over to the fiction and poetry sections, you'll find a tremendous amount of very deep and rich truth conveyed through narrative, metaphors, and powerful imagery rather than literal facts."

That would be an intelligent answer. And you'd have to be a relatively intelligent person to understand it. You couldn't be a silly or superficial thinker.

Something similar can be said about understanding the Bible. According to believers, the Bible is the inerrant and infallible Word of God. Unlike the information contained in an average library, all the information in the Bible is true, but that doesn't mean it is all true in the same way. If you read the section of the Bible known as the Gospels, then yes, you are going to be dealing mainly with historical facts—eyewitness accounts of events that really, truly happened in the life of Jesus. If you go to the book of Genesis, however, you are going to find stories that are every bit as true, but more *allegorical* in nature.

An *allegory* is a story or poem that contains a hidden meaning—usually a moral or religious truth. Thus the meaning of the story of Jonah and the whale is that if you run away from God—as Jonah did—you will be swallowed up in darkness. Yet even in the depths and bowels of a darkness that seems overwhelming, there is always hope that you might once again see the light of day—because as long as you turn back to God, you always have access to forgiveness and salvation.

That is the truth contained in the story—and it is a very great truth. When atheists ridicule the book of Jonah as a moronic myth, they don't prove that the Bible is wrong, that believers are gullible, or that God doesn't exist. All they prove is that they are too shallow and slow-witted to understand more sophisticated ways of reading.

Of course, the story of Jonah goes even deeper than this. Jonah was also a prophet who "prefigured" Jesus Christ. According to the Gospels, Christ suffered a brutal execution and was entombed in the earth for three days before rising from the dead. By his death and resurrection, Christ showed that even the greatest evil—the murder of God—could be overcome and transformed into the greatest good: the gift of eternal life in heaven. Thus, the story of Jonah's captivity in the belly of the fish for three days and his subsequent release *foreshadowed* Christ's burial in the tomb and final victory over death and helped prepare mankind to receive the most important of all religious messages. (Jesus himself read the story of Jonah in this way, Matt. 12:39–41.)

The idea being conveyed in the biblical account of Jonah is therefore very profound. You can reject it if you like, but you certainly can't pretend it's not a weighty theological concept.

And yet that's exactly what atheists do. They read the story of Jonah through a ridiculously narrow lens, discredit the book as scientifically impossible, and then conclude with a colossal non-sequitur: because the Bible is false, therefore God himself is a mere human fabrication.

Absurd!

They do the same thing when it comes to religion. As we saw in chapter 3, atheists make the preposterous claim that religion is the worst enemy of mankind, that it is responsible for most of history's murder and bloodshed. They point out all the bad deeds committed by religious people over the centuries—vices, cruelties, stupidities, hypocrisies—and then conclude not only that religion is evil, but also that belief in God is unreasonable. In other words, they slay the dragon of organized religion and then announce that they have slain God too. That's the whole premise of Christopher Hitchens's best-selling book, *God Is Not Great—How Religion Poisons Everything.*

But Hitchens's book isn't a logical argument against God; it's simply a diatribe against religion and religious people. The very title contains a glaring non-sequitur: for even if it were true that religion "poisons everything," it certainly doesn't follow that "God is not great" or that he doesn't exist. Just as millions of people in the world don't accept the Bible, millions of people in the world don't subscribe to the tenets of any organized religion—and yet still believe in a personal creator.

Or take another example. The book that you're reading right now is all about atheists. We've given dozens of examples that demonstrate the arrogance, ignorance, ruthlessness, intolerance, and shallowness of these unbelievers. But have we once claimed to disprove the atheist *position*? Have we once made the assertion that because atheists are arrogant, there *must*, therefore, be a God? Of course not. All we've done is show that atheists, themselves, are ignorant, ruthless, imbecilic, et cetera. We wouldn't argue that this somehow proves the Bible, Christianity, or theism to be true. If we did, we'd be committing the same kind of logical fallacy as the atheists; we'd be just as shallow as them—and we're not!

Beyond this obvious non-sequitur, atheists haven't been even remotely successful in slaying the dragon of organized religion. As we've discussed, they've had to place huge blinders over their eyes in order to avoid seeing all the good that religion has done throughout history. They've essentially had to force themselves not to recognize the extraordinary contributions to civilization religion has made to culture, politics, education, and the arts.

G. K. Chesterton once said: "The abuses which are supposed to belong especially to religion belong to *all* human institutions. They are not the sins of supernaturalism, but the sins of nature. . . . When people impute special vices to the Christian Church, they seem entirely to forget that the world . . . has these vices much more. The Church has been cruel; but the world has been much more cruel. The Church has plotted; but the world has plotted much more. The Church has been superstitious; but it has never been so superstitious as the world is when left to itself."[4]

The bottom line is that cataloging the bad behavior of believers doesn't prove anything—except perhaps the bad behavior of humanity. It certainly doesn't prove that religion, itself, is bad; and it doesn't go anywhere near proving that believing in God is bad.

Can you imagine if someone tried to make the same argument against science? What if someone said that scientific study should be outlawed because it was "harmful" to mankind? After all, the history of science hasn't been so spotless. Everyone has heard stories about evil Nazi doctors who conducted unspeakable medical experiments on Jewish children in order to advance the scientific cause. Just think about all the detrimental effects science has had over the course of the last hundred years—and the potential harm it might do in the future. Remember, science has given us the atom bomb and the hydrogen bomb; it has given us ballistic missiles and thousands of other weapons of mass destruction. Science has given us the hideous ability to wipe out the entire population of the earth by pressing a few buttons. It has given us the ability to commit the most ferocious acts of terrorism, the most heinous crimes, and inflict the most intense suffering imaginable.

But would it be fair to say that because of its destructive potential, science itself is bad? Or that it should be banned? Or that we should ignore the tremendous good that it has done? How ludicrous would such conclusions be? Yet that's exactly the kind of argument that atheists use against religion.

We can go on and on.

Another laughable argument advanced by atheists is that the theory of evolution disproves God's existence. Evolution, of course, is the process by which organisms change over time as a result of the various physical and behavioral traits that have been passed on from generation to generation because of their ability to aid in the survival of the species. Atheists think this theory somehow explains the mystery of life. They essentially assert that since bacteria evolved into Beethoven, and microbes mutated into Mozart, the universe has no creator. The world itself, they say, is responsible for its own animate life-forms.

But once again, this is a blatant non-sequitur. Assuming that evolution is true—and remember, it is still very much a theory—there is no evidence to suggest that God did not originally create life on this planet and then allow evolution to develop life further. Evolution does not in any way account for how life began, or why. All it explains is how life might have changed. In other words, evolution is a process of operation. It has nothing to do with origination.[5]

Michael Poole, in his excellent little book on the new atheists, illustrates this crucial distinction with an example: If you were alone in your home and noticed that a light in the next room suddenly came on, you might naturally ask yourself, *Who did that?* You might wonder if your spouse had turned on the light, or maybe your child, or maybe even an intruder. All these would be plausible explanations. But if you asked an electrician the question: "Why did the light go on?" and this particular electrician didn't possess too much common sense, he might respond by saying: "The reason the light went on is because an electric current flowing at low pressure transferred energy to the ionized gases in the light bulb, which raised their atoms into a higher energy orbit, and then back down again, causing them to re-emit their energy in the form of radiation, which in turn excited the phosphor coating on the inside of the tube in the bulb, thereby causing it to emit light."[6]

Now what did the electrician do? Did he answer the question: "Who turned on the light?" Or did he actually answer the question: "What is the scientific process by which light is emitted?"

This is exactly what shallow-thinking atheists do when they claim that evolution disproves God. They use long, scientific descriptions to explain the mechanism by which they think life developed and then jump to the irrational conclusion that they have explained the cause of life itself. In philosophical terms, they confuse *process* with *agency*.[7]

Indeed, atheists not only misunderstand evolution; they also misunderstand the whole mental discipline of science. They seem to have no grasp whatsoever of what scientific study actually entails. If they ever bothered to consult a dictionary, they would find that science deals with events, objects, and phenomena that take place within the empirically measurable and observable universe—and that's all. Philosophy and religion, on the other hand, deal with first and ultimate causes.

Now teenagers who are enraptured with scientific technology and haven't given much thought (yet) to the deeper, metaphysical questions of life can be excused for thinking that science explains where the universe came from. But adult atheists who write extremely hostile books composed of sweeping and childish pronouncements cannot be excused.

In fact, the most idiotic atheistic claim in the world is that "there has never been any scientific evidence discovered for God's existence."

Well, of course there hasn't! What kind of evidence are they expecting to find? An enormous fingerprint on the planet Saturn made eons ago by one of the Almighty's divine digits?

Come on! No rational believer thinks God is one of the observable "objects" within his own creation. If there is a God who made the universe, then he certainly stands apart from that universe. He is certainly radically different from that universe. Like any creator, he must necessarily be outside of his creation.

If, for the sake of argument, all the fictional characters in *Hamlet* could magically come together and perform a series of scientific experiments, would they ever be able to locate William Shakespeare within the country of Denmark or anywhere else in the pages of that play? If all the figures in *The Night Watch* decided to scientifically investigate every cubic centimeter of the canvas they are painted on, would they ever discover Rembrandt? If all the ingredients in a chocolate layer cake could somehow conduct an empirical test on all the other ingredients of that cake, would they ever be able to find the baker?

This is the same kind of thinking employed by atheists when they challenge believers to produce scientific evidence for God's existence. It makes no sense. It's a non-sequitur. Another phony straw man. There's plenty of *rational* evidence to show that God created the universe—but that evidence is not scientific in nature. Atheists can't seem to grasp the elementary distinction between these two different kinds of "knowing"; they don't have a handle on either the limits of science or the deeper question of how science fits into the overall scheme of human knowledge.

This is a very serious intellectual handicap. In fact it even has a name. It's called *scientism*, and it means "the reduction of all legitimate knowledge to the scientific form of knowledge."

Every major atheist writer today has fallen under the delusional spell of scientism, and so have their legions of robotic disciples. They all make the same excessive and asinine claim: "If science can't prove it, then it's not real."

But is that true? Is the only kind of reality *scientific* reality?

What about the reality of love or happiness or tragedy or hope? What about the reality of literature or music or art? What about the reality of common sense or intuition? What about the reality of history or reliable testimony? What about the reality of the whole world of the spirit?

Are all of these fake or nonexistent?

The truth is, certain things in life can't be scientifically ascertained. As we said previously, science cannot, has not, and will not ever be able to answer questions such as: Why is there something rather than nothing? Why is there life rather than lifelessness? Why is there thought rather than thoughtlessness?

These questions cannot be answered by science for the simple reason that *they are not scientific questions to begin with*—they are philosophic questions. So it is impossible to use the scientific method to deal with them; impossible to apply empirical observation to them; impossible to perform experiments on them. Science isn't applicable in these cases, just as it isn't applicable when trying to prove or disprove truths about art, literature, music, poetry, and love.

Again, this is a deeper form of thinking—and one that atheists hardly ever engage in. They don't ask themselves, "What are the different kinds of truth knowable by human beings, and does the concept of God fall into one of those categories?" Instead they are content to repeat the same old, sorry litany of non-sequiturs: "The Bible disproves God's existence. Religion disproves God's existence. Evolution disproves God's existence. Science disproves God's existence. The complexity of the universe disproves God's existence. Unanswered prayer disproves God's existence. The large number of intellectuals who are atheist disproves God's existence. The desire for heaven disproves God's existence. The concept of hell disproves God's existence. Suffering disproves God's existence."

But none of these assertions disproves anything. All can be answered rationally and logically. But in order to do that, we must demonstrate not only why they are illogical, but also why the very terms atheists use are incorrect misrepresentations; why they are just phony straw-man arguments. For instance, when atheists say that the Christian concept of hell is so horrible that no one could possibly believe it, the first thing one must do is correct their cartoonish idea of hell. When atheists say that the biblical concept of God is so cruel that no one could possibly accept it, the first thing one must do is correct their naïve notion of God. When atheists say that the large number of unanswered prayers in the world makes it foolish for anyone to pray, the first thing one must do is correct their childish understanding of prayer.

This takes time. It takes thought. It takes work. And unfortunately, atheists aren't willing to put in the intellectual effort necessary to argue on this level. Instead they prefer to waste their time squabbling over irrelevancies.

The question is: Why? Why won't they deal honestly with the real philosophical and theological arguments for God's existence?

Why don't they address, for example, the question of efficient causality (the first, uncaused cause)? Why don't they address the question of infinite contingencies (whether or not the cosmos *must* exist)? Why don't they address the question of the "intelligibility" of the universe? Why don't they address the question of free will and the human soul? Why don't they address the question of intelligent design (which they always dismiss without actually answering)?

We'll be talking about some of these things later on, but the point now is to understand that atheists have utterly failed to engage in a vigorous intellectual discussion about the topics mentioned previously. In fact, most of the angry unbelievers who write their angry books and blogs aren't even able to comprehend these matters, much less debate them. All they seem to care about is knocking down straw men.

What could be their reason?

The answer, I'm afraid, lies in the fact that straw men are easy opponents. Straw men don't have brains. They don't argue back. They don't point out logical fallacies and non-sequiturs. They don't attempt to fight at all—which is exactly why atheists love them so much. At heart, atheists are nothing but dimwitted bullies. And all bullies, deep down, are cowards who are afraid to fight anyone their own size.

But that's a subject we'll be dealing with in our next chapter—the massive yellow streak going straight down the back of the modern atheist movement.

CHAPTER 6

THE COWARDICE OF THE ATHEISTS

There is a spiritual law that applies in a particularly powerful way to the atheists we've been talking about in this book. It can't be proven scientifically, of course, but it is true nonetheless. And the law is this: *you can't practice vice, virtuously.*

If you are engaged in some kind of habitual vice in one area of your life, then sure as the sun rises each day, you are going to be practicing some kind of vice in another area as well. It's possible to compartmentalize your personal and business lives in many different ways, but not when it comes to morality—at least not for long.

If, for example, you are a habitual thief, then it's safe to assume that you are not going to be a very faithful person either. If you're a habitual philanderer, then chances are you're not going to be very honest. If you are a habitual liar, then you're not going to be very wise. It's just a ridiculous Hollywood fantasy to think that someone who sells drugs for a living is also going to be a model citizen and demonstrate heroic virtue in his personal life. Or that a person who works in the pornography industry is going to be a loving, honest, adoring, and faithful spouse. It's not possible over the long term. Pride, gluttony, lust, laziness, lying, and all the other vices are mysteriously connected, just as the virtues are mysteriously connected. Everything is wired together in some way.

People who believe in God might explain this phenomenon in two ways: They might tell you poetically that when you turn away from the light, you will naturally find yourself engulfed in darkness. When you turn away from the good, you will naturally leave behind *all* that is good. From a theological perspective, they might alternatively say that when you engage in habitual vice, you are actually working to erode your willpower. Ultimately your willpower gives you the strength to do good and avoid evil; therefore, if you habitually give in to one particular vice, then your diminishing willpower will no longer be strong and effective enough to battle other vices either.

When your willpower is weakened, you basically lose control everywhere in life. You darken the intellect so that it can't see what's right. You disable the body so it can't fight temptation. You de-energize and immobilize everything. It's like moving your left leg in one direction, and your right leg in the other. When you do that, you're not going to be able to go anywhere. You're going to be stuck in the same position. Or if you're driving in your car and you try to step on the gas with one foot and the brake with the other, you're going to come to a screeching halt—and probably damage your vehicle too.

The bottom line is, your moral behavior in one area affects your moral behavior in another area. If you get stuck in the groove of doing something bad, you'll eventually begin doing other bad things as well. *You can't practice vice, virtuously.*

Enter our friends, the atheists. It's no accident that these folks seem to be so bad in so many different ways. It's not just that they've made a mistake in one area or that they happen to be wrong about one particular question. If that were the case, then all we would have to do is engage in friendly debate. But atheists are not just incorrect in their reasoning about God. As a group, we've already shown them to be arrogant, ignorant, deceptive, ruthless, intolerant, unforgiving, unrelenting, and extraordinarily foolish. And we're only halfway through this book!

When people carry on in such a toxic way for so long, their character traits become quite predictable. It's not difficult to conclude that they will generally be rude, bullying, and boorish across the whole spectrum of social behavior. In the previous chapter, for instance, we discussed how atheists love to fight straw men because straw men can't fight back. This fact is explained by a powerful vice that atheists constantly exhibit: intellectual and physical *cowardice.*

For example, everyone agrees that Christopher Hitchens was one of the foremost atheists of modern times. An excellent writer as well as a funny and quick-witted debater, he was considered a hero by millions of his young atheist followers. But do you know whom Christopher Hitchens named as his most loathsome and despicable enemy?

Mother Teresa—the little saint from Calcutta!

This is not a joke. Hitchens wrote an extremely rude and uncharitable book called *The Missionary Position*[1] in which he unleashed all his atheistic fury on the Catholic nun, known the world over as one of the greatest humanitarians of the twentieth century. Mother Teresa, it will be recalled, founded the Missionaries of Charity, an order of sisters whose primary task is to care for the unfortunate of the world. The sisters provide assistance to the poorest of the poor in Asia, Africa, and Latin America, and undertake relief work in the wake of floods, epidemics, and famines. They have houses, schools, orphanages, hospitals, and hospices in North America, Europe, and Australia, where they take care of lepers, alcoholics, the homeless, and AIDS sufferers.

Mother Teresa herself chose to live and work in the dirtiest slums of India for sixty years. This humble woman, whom Hitchens ridiculed as "Hell's Angel," stood just under five feet high and devoted her whole life to serving the destitute and the dying.[2] She was awarded the Nobel Peace Prize in 1979 and became a global symbol for charitable and selfless work. People of all races, religions, and nationalities recognize the goodness and kindness of this little saint. Yet to Hitchens, Mother Teresa was nothing but a "monster." Why?

Hitchens despised Mother Teresa because, as a Catholic nun, she was against divorce and abortion and artificial contraception; and in Hitchens's atheistic philosophy, these are the only effective methods of combating overpopulation and poverty. Therefore, by opposing the atheist viewpoint, Mother Teresa was guilty of insincerity and hypocrisy. Indeed, Hitchens claimed that the *real* reason the nun worked so tirelessly for the poor was not to help them, but rather to *foster* poverty—which she wanted to spread across the planet for the sole purpose of preserving the institutions she had founded.[3] According to Hitchens, *that's* why Mother Teresa spent thousands of hours caring for the outcasts of society.

My, my.

And yet, to the empty, warped, and bullying brain of the modern-day atheist, this ludicrous theory makes perfect sense. How can it be so?

In an interesting article on bullying from *Psychology Today*, author Preston Ni writes: "The most important thing to keep in mind about bullies is that they pick on those whom they perceive as weaker, so as long as you remain passive and compliant, you make yourself a target. Many bullies are also cowards on the inside."[4]

Cowards on the inside. That explains a lot.

It explains, for instance, why atheists are so vocal in their criticism of committed Christians and yet so mysteriously silent when it comes to radical Muslims. Consider all the anti-Christian books that have been written by atheists in the past few years. We've only mentioned a few so far, such as *God Is Not Great*, *The God Delusion*, *The End of Faith*, and *Letter to a Christian Nation*, but there are hundreds more. For instance:

- *American Fascists: The Christian Right and the War on America*
- *The Baptizing of America: The Religious Right's Plans for the Rest of Us*
- *Atheist Universe: The Thinking Person's Answer to Christian Fundamentalism*
- *All That's Wrong with the Bible: Contradictions, Absurdities, and More*
- *God Needs to Go: Why Christian Beliefs Fail*

To name a few.

But where are all the atheist books warning against the

dangers of Islamic fundamentalism? Where are all the atheist blogs railing against the outrages of Muslim extremists? Do atheists seriously think that Christians pose more of a threat to the United States than Islamic terrorists?

Yes, it's true that some of the new atheists have been critical of Islam—especially Bill Maher—but it's a case of the exception proving the rule.[5] After all, atheist authors have traveled all over America and Europe blasting Christian leaders and values. But how many of them have given the same kind of anti-God lectures in Saudi Arabia, Sudan, Egypt, and the other predominantly Islamic countries? How many of them have debated Muslim scholars in those countries? How many of them have been interviewed on Al Jazeera?

These are the same pompous pundits who have described Jesus Christ and Christianity in the vilest terms imaginable. But how many of them have publicly condemned Allah or Muhammad? These are the same arrogant authors who have regularly lambasted the Christian church for its supposedly anti-women stance. (One atheist writer posted the following lovely sentiment on Facebook: "If Mary had had an abortion, we wouldn't be in this mess!")[6] But how many of them have written scathing books about the far more oppressive anti-women laws prevalent throughout the Muslim world? Remember, under Islamic law, a woman can be stoned to death if she's so much as *accused* of adultery. Yet we hardly hear a peep from atheists about such travesties of justice. Instead they spend their time going after Mother Teresa!

Best-selling author and scholar Rabbi Daniel Lapin believes that the atheist community has made a conscious choice to take this hypocritical approach in their public commentary. "They sit within the comfort and safety of countries based on Christian principles," he says, "and conveniently launch condemnations which are roughly quantifiable as being 90% anti-Christian and 10% anti-other religions (and this may be being too generous an estimation)."[7]

But why? Why do atheists mercilessly mock Christians while at the same time ignoring the more aggressive and egregious actions of Muslims?

One well-known atheist professor—in a rare moment of atheistic candor—admitted the truth. Dr. Phil Zuckerman, who teaches secular studies at Pitzer College in Claremont, California, and also writes a popular blog that criticizes Christianity and Judaism, said in a discussion on religious liberty at Georgetown University:

> I absolutely agree that it is okay for those on the left to critique, mock, deride Christianity, but Islam gets a free pass—which is so strange, because if you care about women's rights, if you care about human rights, if you care about gay rights, then really Islam is much more problematic—sorry to paint Islam with a huge brush—and much more devastating. . . . What keeps me from critiquing Islam on my blog is just fear. I've got three kids . . . I know I can say anything about Christianity or Mormonism and I'm not living in fear.[8]

"As an atheist," Zuckerman said, "where on planet Earth is the death penalty meted out to atheists? It's only in twenty-four Muslim countries. Where have human rights flourished the most? In Christian nations."[9]

There you have it. Even though atheists are as vehemently

opposed to Muslims' belief in Allah as they are to Christians' belief in Christ, they're just too scared to speak out. Atheists in Hollywood, the media, academia, and the publishing world are terrified that Islamic zealots will retaliate against them in a physical way if they say anything too harsh about the Muslim religion. So, instead of voicing their objections, they attack what they consider to be a much softer and safer target—Christianity.

And isn't this exactly the kind of cowardly behavior typical of bullies? Bullies never pick on anyone their own size. They always go after those whom they think will turn the other cheek. It's really quite repulsive. After all, if atheists were half as belligerent to Muslims as they are to Christians, you could at least respect them for having the courage of their convictions—but they're not.

Indeed the whole psychology of the unbeliever is built on fear. We saw in the last chapter that atheists are afraid of real arguments, and instead prefer to do battle with phony straw men of their own invention. They're afraid of history, and instead prefer to remain in a state of profound ignorance. They're afraid of honesty, and instead resort to big lies to defame their opposition. They're afraid of democracy, and instead use ruthless suppression and intimidation as a means of silencing viewpoints that are contrary to their own. Atheists are cowards through and through, inside and out. Theirs is a veritable *culture of cowardice.*

Atheists are even afraid to face the truth about their own philosophy. They delude themselves as to what it truly means to be an atheist. They claim, for instance, that atheism has no bearing whatsoever on their moral behavior.

Not only does this make no sense, but also it counters the history of atheistic thought. One has only to consult the writings of famous atheist philosophers of the past to see how their modern counterparts have chosen a much more timid intellectual path. In fact, the atheists of the nineteenth century would be ashamed and even disgusted with the latest breed of unbelievers.

Men like Friedrich Nietzsche, for example, understood that without God there can be no fixed morality. Without a Supreme Being, there can be no supreme lawgiver—and hence no supreme law. This was a bold, logical, and honest way of thinking, and unlike Hitchens, Dawkins, Harris, and others, the old atheists were not afraid to proclaim it.

In his famous atheist treatise *Beyond Good and Evil*, Nietzsche wrote:

> Severity, violence, slavery, danger in the street and in the heart, secrecy, stoicism, tempter's art and devilry of every kind . . . everything wicked, terrible, tyrannical, predatory, and serpentine in man, serves as well for the elevation of the human species as its opposite. . . . Such kind of men are we, we free spirits! . . . The noble type of man regards *himself* as a determiner of values . . . he is a *creator of values*.[10]

That's what Nietzsche believed atheists should be—free spirits. Spirits who were really free to do whatever they wished, once they had thrown off the shackles of religious "oppression."

In Nietzsche's philosophy, it is permissible to go "beyond good and evil" because without God, there really is no such thing as good and evil. These concepts are merely human inventions. What makes something good or evil is determined solely by whether or not it serves our own personal, practical purposes. That's why Nietzsche urged his followers to become

Übermensch—or Supermen—individuals who could understand that good and evil are simply artificial restrictions imposed by religion in order to prevent the strong from dominating the weak. Indeed, Nietzsche scorned the weak. He embraced an atheistic philosophy of social Darwinism that advocated not only survival of the fittest but also survival of the most powerful.

And why not? If God doesn't exist, how can there be any kind of objective moral law to protect the weak? How can any kind of objective moral law exist at all?

Follow this point closely, because it shows why today's atheists are such intellectual cowards. We're not saying here that atheists can't be good people, or that they can't act in a morally responsible way, or that they can't act to protect the weak. Of course they can. A person doesn't have to accept the existence of God in order to be against killing or lying or cheating.

But that's not the point. An atheist who says it's wrong to kill is voicing his own *personal convictions*, and nothing more. He may find killing repugnant. He may strongly empathize with the suffering of others. He may think that for society to survive, killing must not be permitted. Christopher Hitchens, full of courageous virtue following his attacks on Mother Teresa, defended atheistic morality by saying: "We know that we can't get along if we permit perjury, theft, murder, rape."[11] Therefore, he reasoned, you can be an atheist and still be against the same crimes that believers are against.

And that's right, you can! There are a hundred different reasons for believing that killing is harmful or counterproductive to society, but none of these reasons are *morally binding*. None of them are the logical result of any existential or objective standard of morality. None show that killing is wrong in and of itself.

Therefore, none can serve as a permanent basis for *obligating* people to obey laws against killing.

This lack of moral objectivity explains why there have been so many murderous atheist regimes in the past. If an atheist leader with absolute power wants to act cruelly, he has no binding or transcendent reason not to. Without God, objective morality cannot exist. Only God, who transcends society, can say that human beings *must* act this way or that—*or else* they are breaking a law that is also transcendent. In other words, without a transcendent and almighty Being, there can be no such thing as a transcendent or unbreakable law.

The bottom line is that an atheist may act in a virtuous manner—but not because he *must*. Without God, moral precepts are simply personal codes of conduct. They are tastes or opinions—like what flavor ice cream you prefer—and not objective imperatives that are morally binding on all people.

This is a logical and consistent way of thinking—and the atheists of the nineteenth century understood it. They were serious about their atheism. They didn't coddle and baby their followers by lying to them about the logical implications of their own philosophy.

But the atheists of today don't want to admit that truth. They want to have their cake and eat it too. They go on and on about how morality can be rooted in empathy or the avoidance of suffering or the betterment of society. They go on and on about how atheism has no significant effect on moral behavior. They go on and on about how atheists are just as good and kind and law-abiding as believers. But they don't want to face up to what they really believe: that morality is ultimately relative and based on personal preferences and on expedience.

They don't want to admit that atheism is therefore incapable of sustaining any kind of coherent system of morality—except one based on ruthless power.

Why do atheists refuse to acknowledge these conclusions? Barry Arrington, writing in the blog *Uncommon Descent*, gives the answer: "Because they are simpering cowards!"[12]

You see, it's possible to respect a man like Nietzsche while disagreeing with his beliefs—because he at least followed his premises where they logically led him. But how can a thinking person have anything but contempt for what Arrington calls the "smiley-faced, weak-kneed, milquetoast atheism that insists that God is dead and all is well because we are just as nice as you"?[13]

The truth is that Nietzsche would have spit in contempt on the atheists who are writing books and blogs today. Nietzsche was wrong in his anti-God philosophy, and in the end, became an insane and tragic figure; but at least he was courageous enough to be honest. Modern atheists are not.

Finally, in discussing the atheists' culture of cowardice, we can't fail to mention that atheists today are even afraid of their own human nature. Indeed, they're afraid of basic human psychology and basic human desires. This is a very profound form of cowardice, and one that requires more serious consideration.

Bishop Robert Barron, whom we mentioned earlier, has given an extensive series of talks on the new atheists and has articulated this fear of human nature in the following way:

> Human beings have deep within them a natural desire for things like truth, love, goodness, beauty, faith, and justice. These are not material goods. They transcend the material world. They are, if you will, spiritual in nature.[14]

That's why humans are never truly satisfied with acquiring material things. Even when we have an abundance of possessions—even when we have all the pleasures that this world can offer—we still yearn for something more.

This fact poses a problem for atheists. According to their materialist view of the world, human beings are merely animals. We may be more intelligent than other animals, but we are animals, nonetheless. Now animals, as a rule, are not hard to satisfy. For example, when you give a dog a big bowl of food and a big bowl of water and you play with him for a while, and then give him a nice warm place by the fire to sleep, he is going to be fully content. He is going to be as happy as any dog in the world could be.

But that's not true for human beings. If we were just "dogs with bigger brains," as modern atheists claim, then we would be fully satisfied with lots of money, houses, vacations, sex, and material comforts. Like the dog by the fire, we would fall blissfully asleep once we had our fill of those things and never wish for anything more.[15]

Only we don't feel that way. In fact, it is precisely when we have experienced all the wonderful things the world has to offer that we realize more powerfully than ever before that we still lack something, that we are still *hungry* for something that transcends the world. In such moments, we realize we are not just highly intelligent animals, but rather, we possess some kind of mysterious spiritual component as well.

To those who believe in God, these "transcendent desires" don't pose any problem. Indeed, they make perfect sense. As C. S. Lewis said, the hunger we have for truth, goodness, beauty, et cetera, is really a hunger for God himself. They are just different aspects of God. They are "reflections" of him from different angles, and the yearning we have for them was put there by our Creator for a reason: so that we would seek him. Indeed, God is the "fuel" we were built to run on.[16] Or, as Saint Augustine succinctly summarized, "our hearts are restless" until they rest in God.[17]

The Bible is full of stories about kings who became rich and mighty, yet failed to achieve happiness. As the book of Ecclesiastes famously says, "all is vanity." According to believers, what God is trying to teach us in these stories is that the solution to the riddle of human happiness is not to seek more riches, but rather to change our priorities and reorder our lives so that the transcendent, spiritual values come *first*. Truth, love, goodness, beauty, faith, and justice must come *before* money, sex, power, prestige, possessions, and honor. In other words, God must come first, and everything else after. *That* is the proper perspective for the well-ordered and happy human being. And while these desires can never be *completely* satisfied in this life, human beings can at least look forward to full union with God in heaven, when we will finally be able to enjoy perfect happiness. Therefore, despite any suffering we encounter in this life, we can always have hope for the future.

Naturally, those who don't believe in God reject this way of thinking—but they have a problem on their hands. If there is no God and no spiritual reality, what are these transcendent desires? Where do they come from? Why do we have them? Even more importantly, what does their existence mean for us? What are their implications for our happiness?

And here is where the modern atheists show once again how cowardly they are. Here is where they show how greatly inferior they are to the unbelievers of the past.

The older brand of atheists—especially existentialists like Jean-Paul Sartre and Albert Camus—understood that human beings have deep, inborn desires that cannot be satisfied by anything in this world. They recognized that an inherent tension exists between the desire we have for transcendence—for "God" in some form—and the fact (in their judgment) that God does not exist. They concluded that because of this paradox, life is tragic; indeed, life is an absurdity.[18] After all, what's the point of having desires if they can't ever be fulfilled?

In order to deal with this paradox of absurdity, their solution was to say that human beings needed to boldly assert the power of their own will. Basically, human beings needed to fully *recognize and accept* the futility, tragedy, and meaninglessness of life, and push on anyway—like some stoic Hemingway hero.

Like Nietzsche before them, the existentialist atheists were wrong in their thinking, but at least brave in their approach to life. They tried to accept the implications of their belief, no matter how grim those implications might be. They were serious about their atheism—not frivolous, like today's "smiley-faced, weak-kneed, milquetoast" unbelievers. They were tough enough to admit that human beings *do* have a yearning for the transcendent, and that this desire creates a problem for atheists—a problem that requires a courageous philosophy in response.

The atheists of today, however, do not admit there is a problem. They don't admit human beings have transcendent desires at all. Materialists to the core, they deny any kind of spiritual reality. Instead, they believe the silliness that says science has all the answers—that our deepest longings for love and friendship and beauty and honor and hope and home and eternal life are really just the result of a meaningless movement of molecules.

As Bishop Barron has said, religion has been accused of being "the opiate of the masses." But in reality, it is modern atheism that offers a hallucinogenic drug to its followers—a drug that masks the desires we all have deep within us for something more. "You really don't have those desires," the atheists whisper over and over. "Just relax and enjoy life. There's nothing more than this world. God is an illusion. There's no need to look into yourself and ask difficult existential questions about the spiritual meaning of being. The only thing that counts is science—the only thing that matters is matter."

Even in the face of all the millionaires, movie stars, and music industry celebrities who are so desperately unhappy despite their wealth and worldly fame, these new atheists persist in living in denial. They're just too afraid to face facts about human nature. They're too afraid to be honest about what the human heart really needs to be fulfilled.

Atheists have always claimed that believers are afraid of death, but the truth is, atheists are afraid of *life*.

In the next chapter, we'll see just how far they take this fear of life. For, like everything else they touch, they're not happy unless they distort even this simple emotion into something dark and twisted. Not content to merely "be afraid" and leave the rest of us alone, atheists have taken their fear of life to the extreme and turned it into a morbid, macabre, and murderous love affair with death—a love they insist the whole world share.

CHAPTER 7

THE DEATH-CENTEREDNESS
OF THE ATHEISTS

In the Gospels, Christ identifies himself with life and says of his mission: "I came so that they might have life and have it more abundantly."[1]

In the book of Proverbs, we see that the converse is also true: "All who hate me [God] love death."[2]

This simple but eerie dictum is found throughout Scripture, and we'll discuss it more a little later in this book when we talk about the real motivation at the heart of the atheist movement. For now, though, it's enough to say that there is a profound and fundamental connection between atheism and death.

At first, this might seem illogical. After all, one would think that since atheists do not believe in an afterlife, they would do all they could to prolong *this* life. One would think that because they do not believe in a hereafter, they would do all they could to defend, protect, and treasure life in the here and now.

Alas, this is not the case. Indeed the opposite is true.

At the end of the last chapter we concluded with the provocative remark that atheists have a love affair with death. The truth is even stranger and more frightening, for atheists today lust after death. Their whole outlook is pervaded by death. Their actions drip with death.

Once again, we need to get some historical context in order to understand the morbidly bizarre, death-centered agenda of the modern-day atheist.

We've already talked about the important atheist and anti-Christian philosophers of the eighteenth and nineteenth centuries—men like Voltaire, Rousseau, Marx, Freud, Feuerbach, and Nietzsche. The critical point to grasp about these thinkers is that their writings, while revolutionary, did not permeate into the general culture until after they were dead. The vast majority of people who lived at the time these men were expounding their views remained steadfastly Christian.

In the years following Nietzsche's death in 1900, however, the atheistic philosophy of such thinkers began to find its way into the literature of the nations of the world. People such as Julian Huxley in England, John Dewey in America, Ernst Haeckel in Germany, and Jean-Paul Sartre in France are typical of the philosophers who agreed with the author of *Beyond Good and Evil*—that the Christian faith was the greatest enemy of humanity. Nietzsche's disciple John Dewey, for example, is the recognized father of American education. His fifty books have penetrated every facet of our modern school system.

The point is, atheism today is *not* a minority position—as some would think. On the contrary, in most developed countries, atheistic thinking has already achieved relative dominance.

Granted, not everyone in these societies uses the word *atheist* to describe their philosophy. But that is merely a linguistic point. The popular atheism of both Europe and North America is very much a *practical* form of unbelief. It is not so much the intellectual denial of God—although that is becoming more and more fashionable—but rather the moral exclusion of God from one's life. In other words, while many people stop short of calling themselves *atheists*, they simultaneously reject the majority of dogmas held by Judaism, Christianity, and other world religions.

The bottom line is that whether a culture is called atheistic isn't nearly as important as whether the culture *behaves* in an atheistic way. According to Philip Kuchar:

> A "functional" atheist is someone who behaves as an atheist regardless of any religious beliefs the person may have. . . . The combination of science and technology . . . makes for a functionally atheistic culture, for a culture in which religions have comparatively little relevance. So long as people tend at work and at home to set aside rather than to act on their religious beliefs in any significant way, these people might as well be called atheists even if they don't like the word "atheist." These people are functional atheists, because they live in secular societies in which the prime movers aren't religious institutions, but [secular ones].[3]

For the last century or so, we have lived in a predominantly secular and functionally atheistic society—or at the very least, one that is quickly moving in that direction. The government, the media, the academic world, the entertainment industry, the medical profession, and others have all set aside their religious beliefs in favor of secular values. They are, for all practical purposes, atheistic *in their culture*.[4]

The average Hollywood movie star, for instance, doesn't have a clue about the philosophy of Nietzsche and Feuerbach; but by living a hedonistic lifestyle, by aggressively rejecting Judeo-Christian morality, and by adopting a purely secular system of values, these celebrities are essentially acting as functional atheists.

This is a critically important point to understand, because at the same time the culture has embraced a fundamentally atheist mentality, it has also embraced what has famously been called a "culture of death." This is no mere coincidence. The two cultures are inextricably connected.

The term "culture of death" first entered common usage after Pope John Paul II mentioned it several times in his 1995 encyclical, *Evangelium Vitae* (Latin for "the gospel of life").[5] In this encyclical, John Paul II wrote about the intrinsic value of every human life—which, he said, must be welcomed and loved "from conception to natural death."[6] The encyclical warned that the value of human life was fast eroding, and that modern culture has come to consider human life as merely a means to some other end—such as efficiency or economic productivity or personal convenience—and not solely an end or "good" in itself. The encyclical further warned that we were now in the midst of "a new cultural climate" in which abortion, euthanasia, and other anti-life practices, such as human sterilization, capital punishment, contraception, and embryonic stem-cell research on aborted babies are being justified as "rights" in the name of individual freedom.[7]

Indeed, the pope said that our culture has become deeply

attracted to death. He said that these "crimes against life" are "in a certain sense a war of the powerful against the weak. A life which would require greater acceptance, love and care is now considered useless, or held to be an intolerable burden, and is therefore rejected."[8] This dire situation, he wrote, "ought to make us all fully aware that we are facing an enormous and dramatic clash between good and evil, death and life, the 'culture of death' and the 'culture of life.'"[9]

Essentially, the pope was saying that death has become the "cure-all solution" to the problems of the world. Instead of employing love and care and sacrifice to deal with difficulties (which can be painful for us to do), we now simply choose to kill our problems—literally.

The Catholic Church declared John Paul II a saint in 2014, but many people in today's secular society disagree, dismissing the pope as a "right-wing religious fanatic." Some even call him a monster. (Recall how Christopher Hitchens said the same of that other great saint of the twentieth century, Mother Teresa.) But what is the truth? Was the pope correct in his assessment of the culture—or not?

A quick look at some statistics gives us the answer:

- We saw in chapter three that atheist leaders bear the blame for the vast majority of fatalities caused by war and mass murder in history. Indeed, between the years 1917 and 2007, approximately 148 million people were killed by atheistic political regimes.[10]

- The overall number of murders has increased dramatically as well. The United Nations Office on Drugs and Crime regularly conducts a "Global Study on Homicide," and for the last several years, the average number of intentional homicides in the world has been approximately 450,000 per year.[11]

- The number of suicides is even more shocking. According to the World Health Organization, more than 800,000 people kill themselves annually. The website suicide.org puts the number even higher—at more than a million—with one person taking his or her own life every forty seconds.[12]

- The *New York Times* as well as the American Society for Suicide Prevention report that the suicide rate in the United States has surged to its highest levels in three decades, with nearly 45,000 people dying from self-inflicted causes each year.[13] According to *USA Today*, there is a suicide in this country every thirteen minutes.[14]

Regarding abortion, the statistics are truly horrifying:

- Since the 1960s there have been more than one billion abortions worldwide.[15] That is roughly equivalent to one-seventh the total population of the planet.

- The most recent and conservative studies show the annual worldwide number of abortions to be 12.4 million. However, the Guttmacher Institute, which was originally founded by Planned Parenthood and is now an independent research and policy organization committed to "advancing sexual and reproductive health and rights in the United States and globally," in a May 2016 report, estimated the number of global abortions to be an astounding 56.3 million per year![16]

- In America alone, since the *Roe v. Wade* Supreme Court

decision in 1973, more than sixty million abortions have taken place.[17] This is roughly equivalent to one-third of the entire generation conceived in the United States since abortion was legalized.

- The abortion death toll in the United States is now approximately one million per year.[18]
- New York City has the highest abortion rate in the country. According to a recent Center for Disease Control and Prevention (CDC) Abortion Surveillance Report, New York City reported 69,840 abortions and 116,777 registered births, which means that city's abortion rate is 60 percent of its birth rate.[19]
- It is estimated that 92 percent of all women in the world who receive a prenatal diagnosis of Down's syndrome abort their babies.[20]
- In many countries, laws allow mothers to terminate their unborn children simply because they are the "wrong" gender, that is, not the gender they prefer.[21]
- In some countries, abortion is compulsory for couples who already have the state-allowed number of offspring. In China, for instance, that number had been *one* for many years, but was increased to *two* in late 2015.[22] Horror stories abound of women who had their babies forcibly aborted at seven, eight, and even nine months of pregnancy, because they had violated this law.[23]

No matter your position on the abortion issue, it is an undeniable fact that in the last fifty years—the same time society has become so secularized and atheistic—there has been a historically unprecedented number of terminated pregnancies.

Indeed, the atheist–abortion connection has been established in other ways as well. According to a recent Gallup poll, Americans with no religious attachment—self-proclaimed atheists, agnostics, and those with simply no religious preference—identify themselves as "pro-choice" rather than "pro-life" by a 68 percent to 19 percent margin (49 percentage points).[24] This represents the strongest propensity toward the pro-choice position of any major US demographic group.

At the other end of the life spectrum, during this same "functionally atheistic" era, we have also seen a corresponding worldwide acceptance and legalization of assisted suicides and involuntary euthanasia. For example:

- The use of euthanasia and assisted suicide to prematurely end the life of an adult with a terminal illness is now routine across the globe.
- Euthanasia is increasingly being used on those who are mentally ill.
- Since euthanasia was legalized in the Netherlands in 2002, its use has risen 73 percent, with some twenty-five thousand people killed. "Mobile euthanasia teams" now routinely kill approximately one thousand people per year in their homes.[25]
- In Belgium and the Netherlands, people can choose to die if they have a terminal illness, depression, or just a feeling that their lives are "incomplete." In one case in Holland, a forty-one-year-old man was euthanized with the assistance of his physician because he *couldn't stop drinking.*[26]
- Euthanasia is increasingly being used on children who are terminally ill. It is legal for physicians to euthanize

children at the age of twelve in the Netherlands and minors of all ages in Belgium.[27]

- Recently a family in the Netherlands was cleared of any wrongdoing for holding down an elderly woman who struggled desperately against a doctor's efforts to euthanize her. Her crime, it seems, was wandering around her nursing home at night and exhibiting signs of dementia.[28]

- In the United States, the "right-to-die" movement has grown increasingly more powerful. Six states currently permit euthanasia, and many other states are considering it as well.[29] The favored method of "mercy killing" is the involuntary removal of sustenance from patients—recall the drawn-out, court-ordered death by starvation and dehydration of Terri Schiavo.[30]

- In states where euthanasia is legal, it is increasingly being *encouraged*. Stories abound of people whose own physicians recommend against assisted suicide, only to have other doctors—who know little of the patients' histories—write fatal prescriptions for them. In at least one case in Oregon, a woman's insurance would not pay for her to continue her fight against lung cancer, but helpfully noted that it would pay for assisted suicide. Another man in Oregon was denied a life-extending drug, but was notified that the state health plan would pay to kill him.[31]

Again, no matter where you stand on the issue of euthanasia, there can be no question that these are frightening and dangerous times for anyone who is hospitalized or seriously sick.

Yet prominent atheists are unabashedly vocal and callous about their commitment to an across-the-board, pro-death agenda. When, for example, a woman on Twitter asked leading atheist Richard Dawkins what she should do in the event she became pregnant with a Down's syndrome baby, Dawkins immediately responded: "Abort it and try again. It would be immoral to bring it into the world if you have the choice."[32]

He later elaborated that it was wrong to have the baby "from the point of view of the child's own welfare."[33] Dawkins's reasoning was that the life of someone with Down's syndrome would be too full of difficulties to be worth the effort of the parents. It would be much more humane to kill it. In other words, in Dawkins's view it is an *ethical imperative* to abort a mentally handicapped baby—both for the sake of the world, and for the child's own individual sake.

Many parents of children with Down's syndrome were understandably upset when they heard Dawkins's advice. One father sent a heartfelt public letter to the atheist, which read:

> Perhaps you believe that your position on abortion and down syndrome is logically valid. But I wonder if you're kept awake at night by the revulsion that comes with being the champion of killing.
>
> Suffering is not a moral evil to be avoided. Suffering can have meaning and value. Ask Victor Frankl. Or Mohandas Gandhi. Or Martin Luther King, Jr. Or, if you're willing, ask my children.
>
> I have two children with Down syndrome. They're adopted. Their birth-parents faced the choice to abort them, and didn't. Instead the children came to live with us. They're delightful children. They're beautiful. They're happy. One is a cancer survivor, twice-over. I found that in the hospital, as

she underwent chemotherapy and we suffered through agony and exhaustion, our daughter Pia was more focused on befriending nurses and stealing stethoscopes. They suffer, my children, but in the context of irrepressible joy.[34]

Why is there such a difference in thinking here? Why do atheists like Dawkins believe that this man's children—and all other children like them—should have been aborted rather than allowed to live, even when the parents are willing to love and care for them? How can we make sense of the atheists' preference for death over love, acceptance, and sacrifice?

In order to understand their rationale, we need to dig deeper into the philosophy of atheism.

There are three strains of atheistic thought that keep popping up in these pages. All of them can help to illuminate the atheist approach to subjects like homicide, suicide, infanticide, abortion, and euthanasia. Let's take them one by one.

First, atheists believe that since there is no God, there can be no such thing as objective and eternal values. *Everything* is transient. Yes, there can be "practical" preferences, but nothing truly universal or transcendent. Therefore, the only sensible goals for human beings to strive after are worldly pleasures, conveniences, and the elimination of all suffering. If someone or something happens to stand in the way of the attainment of those objectives, it is perfectly acceptable (and even praiseworthy) to do whatever is necessary to eliminate that threat.

Second, since there is no God for the atheist, no objective and eternal moral law can exist. Without objective moral law, human beings are free to become, again in Nietzsche's phrase, Supermen. Unfettered by silly commandments and the guilt that comes from breaking them, humans are at liberty to make their own laws—that is, whatever laws happen to suit them at the time. They, themselves, can define what constitutes a valuable life, or even *life* itself—defining *people*, *killing*, and *mercy* according to their own standards as they go. For Nietzsche and his atheist followers, the most important value in the world is power. Therefore life is always subordinate to choice, and the choice made by the strong to dominate the weak (who usually stand in the way of pleasure and convenience) is always the correct course of action.

Third, atheists believe that since there is no God, it is nonsense to believe that human beings are made "in the image and likeness of God." Indeed, humans are not special at all; rather, they are expendable animals—essentially monkeys with bigger brains. They possess neither God-given, immortal souls, nor any kind of inherent or infinite dignity. They simply represent one biological animal among many biological animals. Therefore, protecting their existence is not particularly important. Humans can be oppressed by cruel governments, murdered, aborted, and euthanized at any age and for any reason—as long as it serves some "greater practical good" (which, of course, is always determined by whomever happens to be strongest at the moment).

These three primary ideas drive the ethical philosophy of atheism. They are not difficult to understand, yet modern atheists do their best to mislead people about them because the vision of the world they imply is nothing short of terrifying.

Remember what we said in the last chapter about this new breed of atheists. Unlike their predecessors, they *constantly* resort to lies. They have to do this because they are too cowardly to admit the logical implications of their thinking. They understand that the language used by Nietzsche is repugnant to most people. They understand that the three strains of thought described above can be frightening and, if applied correctly, deadly. So instead of boldly proclaiming them, they choose to ignore or deny them or, even worse (like Dawkins), hide behind the falsehood that they are only being "compassionate" to those who are suffering.

And yet, once we look past the lies and try to really grasp the fundamental principles of atheistic thought, the whole culture of death makes perfect sense.

It makes sense, for instance, that the Supreme Court of the United States would take it upon itself to "redefine" what a human person is and legalize abortion—a practice that had been considered barbaric by all peoples and nations for thousands of years. That is the logical implication of atheist thinking, which says we can choose to do anything we like—including "decide" what human life is and destroy the weakest and most vulnerable among us.

It makes sense that institutions like Planned Parenthood would become involved in scandals involving the harvesting and selling of fetal organs and other aborted baby parts.[35] That is the logical implication of atheist thinking—which says that because human beings have no transcendent dignity, we can utilize or discard their bodies in any way that might be profitable to us.

It makes sense that, in the twenty-first century, our society would do everything possible to encourage strength, fitness, diet, and longevity—while at the same time promote euthanasia and abortion for any or no medical reason at all. The "healthy and long life" is the atheists' sole definition of a worthwhile life. In the end, pleasure is their only measure; so naturally, when faced with a person whose life does not conform to that definition—for example, a baby with Down's syndrome, an old man with dementia, a young woman with depression—the society is lightning quick to abort, euthanize, or assist in its suicide. That is the logical implication of atheist thinking—which says that the only thing that counts is the physical and empirical "quality of life." Any talk about the deeper spiritual meaning of suffering, endurance, sacrifice, and joy is just religious nonsense.

You see, once we understand the atheists' philosophy of life, it becomes immediately clear why they have such a love affair with death. It also becomes clear what their agenda is for the future.

And this is where things get really scary: because when it comes to using death as a cure-all for human problems, atheists have only just scratched the surface.

Consider the following:

- Many environmentalists today believe that human activity represents the gravest threat to the planet. An increasing number of them are now saying that the most effective solution to our ecological problems would be to dramatically reduce that threat—through abortion and euthanasia. For example, in 2017, Michael Brune, the executive director of the Sierra Club, stated that abortion is an essential tool in protecting the environment from the "threat of overpopulation."[36]
- In the United Kingdom, Lord Shinkwin—who is disabled—recently gave a stirring speech in the House of Lords, in which he talked about the disturbing trends in

abortion law on the grounds of "disability." He said: "The writing is on the wall for people like me. People with congenital disabilities are facing extinction. If we were animals, perhaps we might qualify for protection as an endangered species. But we are only human beings with disabilities, so we do not."[37]

• Currently, there is a strong push by euthanasia advocates to stop spoon-feeding Alzheimer's patients if they "requested that" in advance. Peter Singer, the well-known atheist and professor of bioethics at Princeton University, believes that doctors should be permitted to lethally inject Alzheimer's patients, even if they never asked to be killed—because they qualify as "non-persons."[38]

These are just some of the latest developments in our "culture of death." They represent the firstfruits of what is to come. After all, if human beings are no more than disposable commodities, abortion, euthanasia, and other methods of killing can be justified for any reason at all—including helping to alleviate overpopulation, immigration, poverty, homelessness, child abuse, and problems concerning race relations.

In fact, if you really want to know the agenda of the new atheists, you only have to look back to the older and bolder atheists of the past, who weren't afraid to speak their minds about what they believed.

Margaret Sanger, for instance—the founder of Planned Parenthood (and listed proudly as a "celebrity atheist and activist" on the website celebatheists.com), said in her book, *Woman and the New Race*: "The most merciful thing that the large family does to one of its infant members is to kill it."[39]

She also laid out the following objectives in an article called "America Needs a Code for Babies." Here's a tiny sampling:

Article 1. The purpose of the American Baby Code shall be to provide for a better distribution of babies . . . and to protect society against the propagation and increase of the unfit. . . . Article 4. No woman shall have the legal right to bear a child, and no man shall have the right to become a father, without a permit. . . . Article 6. No permit for parenthood shall be valid for more than one birth.[40]

Ms. Sanger, whose magazine's slogan was "No Gods, No Masters," was an early proponent of eugenics—the science of "improving" the human population by controlled breeding for the purpose of increasing the occurrence of "desirable" characteristics and decreasing the "negative" traits in people. (Recall this was one of the Nazis' favorite fields of study.)

Sanger—still very much celebrated today as a heroine by Planned Parenthood—was not timid at all in proclaiming her belief that human reproduction had to be forcibly controlled and manipulated in order to weed out any undesirables.

In her book *The Pivot of Civilization*, she wrote that handicapped people, including the blind, deaf, dumb, mute, insane, and epileptic, represented the "dead weight of human waste."[41] In her view, we should "apply a stern and rigid policy of sterilization, and segregation to that grade of population whose progeny is tainted or whose inheritance is such that objectionable traits may be transmitted to offspring. . . . The whole dysgenic population [people with 'bad genes'] would have its choice of segregation or [compulsory] sterilization."[42]

Sanger also considered blacks to be an inferior race that had to be sterilized, controlled, and aborted out of existence. She stated:

> If we can train the Negro doctor at the Clinic he can go among them with enthusiasm and with knowledge, which, I believe, will have far-reaching results among the colored people. . . . The ministers [sic] work is also important and also he should be trained, perhaps by the Federation as to our ideals and the goal that we hope to reach. We do not want word to go out that we want to exterminate the Negro population and the minister is the man who can straighten out that idea if it ever occurs to any of their more rebellious members.[43]

This is a particularly chilling quote, given the fact that today Planned Parenthood is extraordinarily active in African American communities. Indeed, a recent study by the group Protecting Black Life found that 79 percent of Planned Parenthood's surgical abortion facilities are located within walking distance of African American neighborhoods.[44] In fact, African American babies in New York City have a better chance of dying in the womb than of being born, according to a report from the New York City Department of Mental Hygiene. On average, for every thousand black babies born in New York City every year, twelve hundred are aborted.[45] In Mississippi, 72 percent of the total number of abortions are performed on black babies—this in a state where whites "outnumber blacks by a ratio of 1.6-to-1."[46]

Margaret Sanger would undoubtedly be thrilled to know that her atheistic vision of a eugenically engineered society is at last coming true.

And then there is infanticide. We can't end this discussion without talking briefly about the killing of babies *that have already been born.*

In the Netherlands, this gruesome practice is already legal. Indeed, it is perfectly acceptable there for doctors and parents to jointly decide that "desperately ill" newborns can be killed shortly after birth. Likewise, "postnatal abortion" (as it is euphemistically called) for disabled children is now being considered in Canada. Udo Schuklenk, the well-known Canadian bioethicist, has stated: "Once we have concluded that death is what is in the best interest of the infant, it is unreasonable not to bring about this death as painlessly and as much controlled in terms of timing by the parents as is feasible."[47]

And why shouldn't they think it "unreasonable" to bring about the death of newborns? If you redefine *person* as only those beings who are capable of rational thought and self-reflection, then not only are fetuses and embryos *not* persons, but neither are infants.

Atheist professor John Harris, perhaps the most highly respected member of the British Medical Association's ethics committee, wholeheartedly agrees. On numerous occasions, he has stated that infanticide is "justifiable" because it is simply not "plausible to think that there is any moral change that occurs during the journey down the birth canal."[48]

In other words, there is no moral difference between aborting a fetus and killing a baby.

Atheist researchers Alberto Giubilini and Francesca Minerva add to the chorus of unbelievers calling for the legalization of baby killing. In their paper, "After-Birth Abortion: Why Should the Baby Live?," they make the following argument:

1) Both fetuses and newborns do not have the same moral status as actual persons; 2) the fact that both are potential persons is morally irrelevant; and 3) adoption is not always in the best interest of actual people."

Therefore, they conclude: "after-birth abortion" (killing a newborn) should be permissible in all the cases where abortion is—including cases where the newborn is not disabled.[49]

All cases . . . including where the newborn is not disabled.

Are you reading these words carefully? They are not made up. They are not the product of religious paranoia. They come from the mouths of some of today's leading atheists. This is where our culture is going. This is where the new atheists are taking us: to a world where ending life is the answer to every problem; a world where killing is always preferable to love and sacrifice; a world where eugenics, abortion, fetal harvesting, euthanasia, assisted suicide, forced suicide, and infanticide are all practiced, all the time, for all reasons. This is the future!

We have to wake up and face facts. If the Bible says that God's primary motive is to bring forth life, then the dark, twisted, and morbid motto of the modern atheist movement is just the opposite: *"We have come that you may have death, and have it more abundantly."*

And as we shall see in the next chapter, not only are the atheists deadly serious about making their ghoulish vision a reality, but they have all the faith and religious fervor necessary to accomplish it.

CHAPTER 8

THE FAITHFULNESS OF
THE ATHEISTS

B elievers have always claimed that atheism not only *takes* faith, but *is* a faith.

Atheists, of course, scoff at this notion, just as they scoff at everything believers say. When it comes to rational argument, atheists will ridicule, mock, jeer, sneer, scorn, dismiss, deride, and hide. They'll do anything except argue rationally.

And that's a pity. Because the assertion that atheism requires faith is a fascinating paradox that deserves discussion. When believers make that claim, they mean it. They're not being facetious in any way. They know what they're talking about because it's their *business* to know about faith. They know the difference between *belief* and *knowledge*.

Atheists do not.

Of course they *say* they do. In fact, atheists make the

ridiculous claim that they have no beliefs whatsoever regarding God. They say that they merely "lack" belief in him. In other words, they define *atheism* not as something positive, but rather, something negative—as the "absence" of belief; an absence that is due to a lack of evidence.

And isn't that so convenient? If atheism were merely the absence of belief, then atheists would never have to defend their position. After all, if a position is really a *non*-position, there is no corresponding intellectual obligation to respond to any criticism of it. And that's what atheists love most: a phony, straw-man non-discussion.

It makes perfect sense. If you're ignorant, shallow, and cowardly to begin with, the last thing you want to do is to defend your thinking on rational grounds. Better to avoid intellectual debate altogether and stick to what you know best—taunting, sneering, and scoffing.

But they're not going to get away with that here. If this book has shown anything at all, it's that atheism is the furthest thing in the world from an absence of belief.

Indeed, atheism is a whole *system* of beliefs—a system that has its own philosophy (materialism), morality (relativism), politics (social Darwinism), and culture (secularism). It even has its own sacraments (abortion, infanticide, and euthanasia). And this system of beliefs has been responsible for more death, carnage, persecution, and misery than any system of beliefs the world has ever known.

So, no, atheists won't get off scot-free by calling what they so fervently believe "mere unbelief." They can't hold out their hands in mock innocence, feigning protest that they have nothing to prove when those same hands are dripping with so much blood. They are going to be held to the same intellectual standard that they claim applies to people of faith.

But before we get to the specifics of what atheists believe, let's first talk a little about faith itself. What, exactly, is this mysterious thing, and why do atheists treat it as such a dirty word?

Essentially, faith is trust or confidence in something that has a strong basis in reason but which can't be *absolutely, empirically proven*. Faith is completely antithetical to superstition and fantasy, which have no rational basis whatsoever. Thus you can't compare it to the belief in Santa Claus or the tooth fairy or "the flying spaghetti monster," as so many atheists frivolously claim. True faith is *always* based on reason.

Contrary to what atheists say, *all* human beings have faith of some kind. It's impossible to live in this world without it. For instance, every morning millions of people get up and drive to work. During their commute, nothing separates them from oncoming traffic except a thin white line. They pass all kinds of cars and trucks and trailers that are going more than sixty miles an hour and headed right toward them. They don't know the drivers of those vehicles. They have no clue about their driving records or whether or not any of them has a drinking problem. If just one of those other drivers swerved a few feet, a crash would occur. Yet these commuters go merrily along without blinking as hundreds of vehicles whiz past them. How can they do that? They have *faith* that those other drivers will stick to their side of the road.

When these folks get to work, it's the same story. They sit down at their desks, and above them is a big ceiling. They haven't ever inspected it. They haven't checked to see if the support beams are nailed in properly or if the wood has been eaten away by termites. They haven't checked to verify that all the building permits are in order. For all they know, the whole structure might suddenly collapse and crush them. And yet day after day they sit in front of their computer screens without a care in the world. Why? Because they have *faith* that the people who built their offices were professionals who did everything they were supposed to do to make sure their working environment was safe.

Almost all our knowledge of history is based on faith too. Think about it. Were you around when the Romans conquered Carthage in 146 BC? Or when Columbus discovered America in 1492? Or when George Washington crossed the Delaware River in 1776? If you didn't actually see those events, how can you be so sure they ever took place?

Oh, but there's "evidence," you say. There are documents and books and testimonies and paintings. Yes, that's right. And that's the same kind of "evidence" on which people of faith base many of their religious beliefs. Whether you're talking about religion or the historical record of mankind, most of the information we have has been passed down to us from generation to generation. Very little of it is firsthand. Very little of it is scientifically provable. Most of it must be accepted on faith— faith in the authors of the documents, faith in the reliability of eyewitnesses, and faith in our ability to draw logical and rational conclusions from a whole range of data and evidence.

The point is, faith is not some fanatical, fundamentalist, ultra-religious concept. It's a *basic necessity* for living in the world. And whether or not atheists admit it, they're just as dependent on it as everyone else.

What are some of the things that atheists take on faith? G. K. Chesterton once said: "When a man stops believing in God he doesn't then believe in nothing—he believes *anything*."[1]

How true that is! There aren't enough pages in this book to describe all the faith-based beliefs that atheists hold dear to their hearts. But let's start with the most obvious—the assertion that God doesn't exist because there is no *evidence* for his existence.

This is, of course, patently absurd. In chapter 1 of this book we discussed some of the great thinkers in history who were also fervent believers. Those men and women had faith in a Supreme Being, not only because of their acceptance of the Bible as the Word of God, but also because of thoughtful, logical, and analytical reasoning. Indeed, there are dozens of rational arguments that demonstrate the existence of God—far too many to go over here. There is the cosmological argument, for instance, which explores the question: "Where did everything come from?" There is the teleological argument, which points to the order and harmony of the universe and asserts that there must be some kind of designer. There are arguments that stem from notions of "contingency," from "desire," from "degrees of perfection," from "miracles," from "morality and conscience," and from "reliable testimonies." The list goes on and on.

All of these are based on logic, on observation of the physical world and our own consciousness, or on inductive and deductive reasoning. None of them are based on Scripture. None of them attempt to prove God's existence merely by asserting that "the Bible says this or that."

The truth is, when atheists say there is no evidence for God, what they really mean is that there is no "scientific evidence" for his existence. That is an altogether different thing. For atheists to even make that claim demonstrates a belief in the power of science that is both exaggerated and irrational. Indeed, the assertion that something must be scientifically explicable or provable in order to be believed is, in itself, an *article of faith*.

This belief, as we noted in chapter 5, is an intellectual fallacy known as *scientism*. It means "the reduction of all legitimate knowledge to the scientific form of knowledge," and its fundamental problem, of course, is that it can't be proven scientifically. There is simply no way to empirically observe or experimentally verify the notion that truth can only be arrived at through scientific means. The whole proposition is therefore unscientific. It is an atheistic belief based solely on their faith in its truth—not on any scientific evidence.

Indeed, the whole study of science would be impossible unless we made another huge unscientific assumption. We must first assume that the universe is *intelligible*—that it is understandable, that it is predictable to some degree, that it obeys the laws of reason, that it "makes sense."

Predictability and obedience to physical laws comprise the cornerstone of scientific inquiry. Without intelligibility, no scientific discussion could take place because you would never be able to trust the outcome of any of the experiments you conducted. You would also never be able to trust your own thought process or reasoning ability. And yet the whole concept of intelligibility has not itself been scientifically proven. At its core, it is a faith-based assumption—a belief based on what *appears* to be the truth.

Now again, there's nothing wrong with this. Like the other kinds of faith we've talked about, it's a necessary part of life. But atheists don't have the courage, honesty, or intelligence to admit it. Instead, they robotically rattle off the same self-delusional drivel: "If it can't be scientifically proven, it's not true."

And that's only the beginning of their faith. Remember,

atheists believe that everything in life has a *purely material* basis. They completely deny the existence of the spiritual. They believe that our thoughts, dreams, passions, loves, hates, hopes, ambitions, virtues, sins, and sufferings are driven solely by atomic activity. They believe that all our philosophies, politics, cultures, art, literature, music, history, and deepest desires for eternal life and all that is transcendent in the world—the good, the true, and the beautiful—is purely the result of biochemical reactions and the random movement of molecules in an empty and lifeless ether.

This is not science; it's faith. What's more, it's an irrational faith that serves as the foundation for all superstition.

But there's even more. Atheists make a whole slew of assumptions that can't be proven scientifically. For instance, they believe that this incredibly complex universe of ours—a universe of unparalleled beauty, harmony, and order—came about all by itself, out of nothing. They believe that organization came out of chaos, that life came out of lifelessness, that consciousness came out of non-consciousness, that reason came out of irrationality.

None of these beliefs can be shown empirically. None can be demonstrated or replicated scientifically. None of them even makes sense.

Of course some atheists—the philosopher David Hume, for example—have denied that the universe is organized to begin with, and some very silly atheists still think that evolution some-how explains how life first began.[2] But these beliefs are utterly unbelievable.

To claim that the universe is chaotic and disorganized flies in the face of common sense. For instance, we all know that the moon orbits around the Earth in a perfect spiral, and the Earth circles the sun in a perfect spiral, and the sun circles the galaxy's center in a perfect spiral.[3] Billions of stars in billions of galaxies all move in similar and predictable spiral paths and with fixed trajectories. Ninety percent of the observable matter in the universe acts in this highly organized way.[4] To deny that the universe is organized is preposterous. Even a high school student with a telescope can see that!

And as to the claim that evolution explains the origin of life, we've touched on this nonsensical notion before. The statistical odds that even the most elemental kind of life could arise as the result of a random mixing of molecules in some primordial "soup" are so astronomical that even scientists have trouble figuring them out. They can't say that the odds are trillions to one, because that figure is much too low!

Dr. Stephen C. Meyer, director of the Center for Science and Culture of the Discovery Institute, argues that the probability of generating even a "short functional protein," which is the simplest building block of life, is 1 in 10^{125}—a number so infinitesimal as to defy description. (It actually means one in one hundred quadragintillion!)[5]

To use a familiar analogy: if you took thousands of letters of the alphabet, threw them high up into the air, watched them all fall to the ground, and they somehow formed themselves into Tolstoy's *War and Peace*, that would be as likely to occur as life being formed by the chance mixing of molecules.

That's why Dr. Meyer and his colleagues have concluded that there is a much greater probability of the existence of some kind of cosmic designer who engineered the creation of life on this planet. They say, "The complex but functionally specified sequences . . . in DNA imply the past action of an intelligent mind, even if such mental agency cannot be directly observed."[6]

Yet despite the testimony of many respected scientists and mathematicians, atheists obstinately refuse to accept even the *possibility* that the universe had a designer. They steadfastly maintain the dogma that life on this planet had to come about by chance. Their position contradicts logic, contradicts experience, and even contradicts science itself. Yet they still believe it. That takes faith.

Let's put it another way. Atheists scoff at Christians for believing that Christ could raise people from the dead because, according to their way of thinking, miracles aren't scientifically possible. But Christians accept the notion that Christ could raise people from the dead only because they also believe that Christ is God, and God is the supernatural Creator of life. That belief requires faith, but at least it has a logical basis. Atheists, on the other hand, believe that life came from non-life, consciousness came from non-consciousness, and thought came from non-thought. Those are much more stupendous miracles than any the Gospels report, but atheists won't concede they are miracles. Their faith is so restrictive that it doesn't allow for the slightest deviation from the doctrine of materialism.

The famous Christian writer and ex-atheist, C. S. Lewis, once said:

> If you are an atheist you do have to believe that the main point in all the religions of the whole world is simply one huge mistake. If you are a Christian, you are free to think that all those religions, even the queerest ones, contain at least some hint of the truth. When I was an atheist I had

to try to persuade myself that most of the human race have always been wrong about the question that mattered to them most; when I became a Christian I was able to take a more liberal view.[7]

A "more liberal view" is something that is not open to atheists. They insist—solely on the basis of faith—that science will one day be able to explain all the mysteries and miracles of the universe.

But science can't even figure out how to make a blade of grass!

In fact, science can't even answer the most basic *scientific* questions. What is dark matter, for example? Or what is dark energy—which can't be seen or felt but somehow takes up 70 percent of the universe?[8] Or how can light be made of both particles and waves at the same time?[9] Or why does time only go in one direction?[10] Or why can we only imagine three dimensions, when so many more are suggested by string theory and other scientific theories?[11] Or how can quantum mechanics and gravity live together?[12] Or how can either one of them exist when black holes contradict both?[13]

These are legitimate scientific mysteries—and scientists don't have a clue as to their answers. Yet atheists continue to worship at the feet of science as though it is some kind of deity, propagating the mad illusion that it holds the key to unlocking all the secrets of the universe.

The truth is, when it comes to the deepest mysteries of life, science will *never* have the answers. The reason we can be so sure is that questions having to do with the origin of the cosmos are *philosophic* in nature, not scientific. Elsewhere in this book we quoted Albert Einstein, who said, "The most beautiful emotion we can experience is the mystical." The deeper we go into science, the more mysterious and mystical things become.

And at its center lies the greatest mystery of all: the mystery of existence.

Why is there something rather than nothing? That is the question of questions, the riddle of riddles, the enigma of enigmas. And atheists are completely in the dark about it.

Let's pause here and really consider this point. It's crucial that we try to understand it because it explains why atheists actually need *more* faith than believers.

Logic and common sense dictate that something can't come from nothing. That much should be obvious to anyone. Therefore, the substance that makes up the cosmos—matter—couldn't have popped into existence spontaneously and by itself. There had to have been some original *cause* for it.

That's why the big bang theory (which, remember, was originally formulated by a Catholic priest) actually strengthens the argument for God's existence. For if the cosmos really did come about as a result of a massive explosion, then what kind of substance or force existed right before that explosion? What precipitated the explosion in the first place?

Only the most ignorant of atheists would believe that nothing existed before the big bang. If they truly thought such a thing, they would be admitting that some kind of God "ignited" the blast (because, again, something can't come from nothing). Thus, any atheist with scientific sense must recognize that the big bang theory only provides a possible explanation for how the *present* universe came about and might have developed. It does not give us any indication of the *origin* of the cosmos.

Now, some scientists have postulated that gravity or some other "force of nature" caused everything to come into being.[14] Other scientists have postulated the existence of a "multiverse," which contained an inconceivably large number of universes that spontaneously created itself (again, a theory for which there is no experimental or observational evidence).[15] But none of these explanations addresses the *original* cause of those forces or that multiverse. None of them addresses the central question of existence itself. Any possible cause scientists theorize about must necessarily have been "contingent" on some other cause, which was also contingent on something else, continuing back in an infinite regress of contingent causes. (Gravity, for example, had to come from somewhere.) Therefore, none of these causes can be the true, original cause.

The bottom line is, everything points back to some mysterious reality that is *not* contingent or dependent on anything else: some timeless reality whose very nature is "to be," some reality that can be defined as "existence itself." Those atheists who have the brainpower to grasp this concept understand that this mysterious, noncontingent reality has only one of two possible identities. Either it is God, whose nature is spiritual, or the cosmos, whose nature is material. In other words, either God or the cosmos *always* existed. There is no other choice.

What does this mean for atheists?

It means they have a big problem on their hands! It means they need faith! It means that, according to their own belief system, the cosmos has no beginning. Matter, itself, has no beginning. In other words, despite the fact that atheists don't believe in an eternal god, they still have to contend with the monumental mystery of *eternal matter*—a mystery that science can never hope to fathom.

After all, how in the world can matter have no beginning? How can *anything* have no beginning? This is something even the greatest scientific geniuses can't wrap their minds around. It's not something that can be dismissed nonchalantly, as so many dull-witted atheists do today.

Those who believe in God have the same mystery to contend with, but at least they have a rational foundation to grab hold of. They assert that it's possible for God (the Creator of the cosmos) to have no beginning only because he is *supernatural* and *spiritual*; because he exists on a whole different plane than the material universe; because it is his *nature* to be transcendent and noncontingent.

The cosmos, on the other hand, does not display the nature of something that is eternal, necessary, and noncontingent. The cosmos could conceivably be much different from what it presently is. It could conceivably operate under different physical laws and be made up of different kinds of universes and even different kinds of particles. Therefore, the nature of the cosmos is not "to be," but rather "to *might* be."

In other words, the cosmos doesn't possess the properties that are consistent with an eternal, noncontingent reality that has no beginning.

God, however, fits the description to a T. According to believers, God is a necessary, unchangeable spiritual being whose very nature is to exist. Recall the profundity of the Bible here. When God finally revealed his name to the Israelites, he said, mysteriously, "I am who am," which basically translates into "I am existence itself." In other words, when God was asked the deepest of all philosophic questions, he responded perfectly!

Moreover, the qualities ascribed to God by theologians

explain the other great mysteries we see in the cosmos. For instance, the intelligence of God explains the order and intelligent design of the universe. The life of God explains the consciousness and life of the biological creatures in the universe. The spiritual nature of God explains the transcendent and spiritual qualities we observe in the universe.

In a word, God is a key that fits *all* the locks.

Now of course none of this provides *absolute proof* that God exists. But as the philosopher Mortimer Adler argued, we at least have "reasonable grounds for affirming God's existence."[16] And those reasonable grounds, in turn, give us a rational basis to take the next steps in the spiritual journey—which include investigating the truth of revelation, the power of prayer, the workings of grace, the writings of the great theologians, and the life and words of Christ—all with fair, objective, and open minds.

Atheists do not have such grounds. At the heart of their belief system is a colossal, unsolvable mystery, about which they must have a blind and baseless faith—a faith that says the cosmos "is what it is" for no reason at all and against all reason. In the end, atheists actually require more faith than believers because their faith involves a much more significant suspension of logic and common sense.

It is this "greater" faith that probably accounts for the aggressive behavior of modern atheists. Faith, after all, is an incredible source of power. It explains why atheists are so militant and fundamentalist in their rhetoric. It explains their breathtaking arrogance and their zealous attempts to suppress all forms of public religious expression. The fact is, atheists today aren't just trying to defend an intellectual position; they're attempting to spread a religion of their own. And though they object when believers apply the word *evangelical* to them, that term describes them perfectly. An evangelical atheist is one who not only believes there is no Supreme Being but also is obsessed with persuading the whole world of this dogma.

And isn't this exactly the kind of obsession we've seen on display throughout this book? Haven't we spoken at length about the obnoxious proselytizing of atheists like Richard Dawkins, whose oratory is every bit as fire-and-brimstone as any fundamentalist preacher, and who routinely makes bombastic statements, such as: "Faith is one of the world's great evils, comparable to the smallpox virus but harder to eradicate"?[17]

"Eradicating" God from the face of the earth is precisely what the new atheists have in mind. And this goal has led believers to assert that atheism is not simply a refusal to accept God, but rather a paradoxical religious creed with two main doctrines: (1) There is no God, and (2) I hate him!

But such quips, though amusing, only serve to trivialize the severity of the atheists' faith. Indeed their bigotry has become so hypocritical that even a few fair-minded atheists have taken notice and voiced their objection. Chris Stedman, for instance, writing in the *Huffington Post*, quoted fellow atheist Reza Aslan at length:

> There is . . . something peculiarly evangelistic about what has been termed the new atheist movement. . . . It is no exaggeration to describe the movement popularized by the likes of Richard Dawkins, Daniel Dennett, Sam Harris, and Christopher Hitchens as a new and particularly zealous form of fundamentalism—an atheist fundamentalism. The parallels with religious fundamentalism are obvious and startling:

the conviction that they are in sole possession of truth (scientific or otherwise), the troubling lack of tolerance for the views of their critics (Dawkins has compared creationists to Holocaust deniers), the insistence on a literalist reading of scripture (more literalist, in fact, than one finds among most religious fundamentalists), the simplistic reductionism of the religious phenomenon, and, perhaps most bizarrely, their overwhelming sense of siege: the belief that they have been oppressed and marginalized by Western societies and are just not going to take it anymore.[18]

That really says it all. Atheists today are simplistic, militant, intolerant, dogmatic, evangelistic, and irrational in their faith. In short, they exhibit all the characteristics that have always been attributed to the "evil" side of religion.

There is, however, one tremendous difference between the evangelistic faith of the believer and that of the modern atheist. Those who believe in God want to spread the good news that God is not just a noncontingent, self-existing reality, but also a personal Being who entered history and became one of us in the form of a humble carpenter from Nazareth. They want to spread the good news that this God loves us and cares about us; that, despite all the suffering in the world, death does not have the final word, but rather, the end of the human story is life—*eternal life*.

If all that is true, then it is indeed good news that should be disseminated far and wide.

The evangelical faith of the atheist, on the other hand, is quite the opposite. At the end of their belief system is death—the death of absolutely everything. One would think they would be content to keep their faith in this gloomy philosophy of futility to themselves and leave the rest of us alone. But they're not. Instead, they have taken their belief in nothingness and turned it into a twisted and inverted gospel, which they want to spread to the ends of the earth.

What can it all mean? We've gone through eight chapters of this book, and it's still not clear.

What is this strange philosophy of unbelief? This *thing* that is so full of pride, arrogance, and false ignorance; this thing that lies, hates, and kills so much? This thing that is in love with death and has more blind faith than all the religions it despises? This thing that wants so desperately to spread its tentacles across the globe?

Even more importantly, what is its ultimate motive and aim?

And here at last we come to the moment of truth, when all questions will be answered. In Dante's *Inferno*, there were nine circles in hell—each worse than the last, each with its own particular form of infernal torture. We have now passed through all the major rings that make up this hellish belief system known as atheism. We have finally arrived at its fiery center and core.

CHAPTER 9

THE MALEVOLENCE OF
THE ATHEISTS

Abandon Hope, All Ye Who Enter Here

The inscription on the sign over the entrance gate to Hell.
CANTO III, *THE INFERNO*, BY DANTE ALIGHIERI

We've just looked at how the new atheists possess an almost evangelistic fervor when it comes to spreading their belief system. If recent studies are to be believed, there is increasing evidence that their efforts are paying off.

Surveys show that atheism is growing at an alarming rate across the globe. In a very short time, countries such as France, the Netherlands, New Zealand, the United Kingdom, and Australia will lose their Christian majorities to those who consider themselves atheists or "religiously unaffiliated." In fact, a recent *National Geographic* article entitled "The World's Newest Major Religion: No Religion" states that the "religiously unaffiliated" is now the second largest "religious group" in Europe.[1] In the United States, it makes up almost a quarter of the population, and in the past decade alone, it has overtaken the Catholic Church, the mainline Protestant denominations, and all followers of non-Christian faiths.

And in truth, these figures understate the impact of atheism on the culture. Recall that earlier in this book we discussed how many people stop short of calling themselves "atheist" while simultaneously rejecting the majority of dogmas held by Judaism, Christianity, and the other world religions. In other words, their professed religious views have little or no relevance in their lives. They are believers in name only; in their behavior, they are thoroughly secular. Therefore, for all practical purposes, they are atheists even though surveys and polls do not categorize them as such.

The bottom line is, despite many pockets of "religious resistance," we live in a functionally atheistic society wherein secular values have achieved dominance in most sectors of the general public—and to an especially high degree in the media, academia, the entertainment industry, and the government. Indeed, in the 150 years since Nietzsche made his bold proclamation that "God is dead," atheists have worked overtime to make his prophecy come true.

But what can we say about the practical results of all this atheistic fervor? What have been the fruits of this fierce philosophy of death and nothingness?

We've talked at length about all the wars and persecutions

and mass murders of the past century; all the abortions and suicides and "mercy killings"—in short, all the evidence that the culture of atheism is a culture of death. But we've only just scratched the surface. The self-centered and hopeless philosophy of atheism has touched every facet of life. Indeed, a recent Harris Poll reported that only one in three Americans consider themselves "happy."[2]

This is astonishing, considering how many advances there have been in technology and medicine. After all, if life is so much more convenient and comfortable than ever before, why hasn't there been a corresponding rise in contentedness? Why, rather, has there been a dramatic increase in the level of overall anguish?

Why are there record numbers of divorces, nervous breakdowns, and stress-related illnesses? Why are the incidents of violent crime, domestic violence, child abuse, sexual abuse, rape, drug addiction, alcoholism, and depression at all-time highs? Why do 350 million people worldwide suffer from depression and other forms of anxiety?[3]

Why is there so much *misery* amid all the technological and economic wealth of the modern era?

"But hold on," comes the atheist response. "Things are so much better now than they used to be. Just look at the tremendous advances we've had in civil rights and women's rights since the rise of secularism."

And indeed that's true. There have been some important and necessary societal improvements—but no thanks to atheists, who were conspicuously absent during the most critical years of those struggles.

Do atheists really need to be reminded that the most heroic leaders of the civil rights movement believed in God? Dr. Martin

Luther King Jr. was a Baptist minister. Malcolm X was a black Muslim. Both boldly proclaimed that their faith in God gave them the strength, courage, and wisdom to take up the civil rights cause—even to the point of sacrificing their lives.[4] Indeed, all the great civil rights figures of the 1960s were believers—Rosa Parks, Ralph Abernathy, Elijah Muhammad, even John F. Kennedy.

The women's rights movement was no different. Before it was hijacked by the abortion-crazed, eugenicist monsters of Planned Parenthood, most of the first feminists were ardent believers. Check the biographies of the leading suffragists in American history and see for yourself. Women like Susan B. Anthony, Sarah F. Norton, and Victoria Woodhull not only believed in God but also were pro-life. (And why not? Why must the road to a woman's freedom be paved with the bodies of unborn babies?)

It was only much later on, when we get to that part of feminist history that involves the mass killing of unborn children, that we see atheists like Gloria Steinem taking center stage.

So, yes, there have been many wonderful advances in human rights over the past hundred years, but they have come about mainly as a result of the blood, sweat, and tears of believers—*not* unbelievers. When we speak of the growing malaise and hopelessness of modern-day society, *that* has been the contribution of the atheists.

G. K. Chesterton once called atheism the "most daring of all dogmas" because it asserts something fundamentally contrary to human nature: a "universal negative."[5] That negative spirit is what lies behind so much of the gloom prevalent today. In his book *The Real Face of Atheism*, Ravi Zacharias explains:

> Having killed God, the atheist is left with no reason for
> being, no morality to espouse, no meaning to life, and no

hope beyond the grave. Significantly, the absence of future hope has an amazing capacity to reach into the present and eat away at the structure of life, as termites would a giant wooden foundation. Hope is that indispensible element that makes the present so important. . . . There is a complete sense of alienation in the world one hundred years after Nietzsche. It is this utterly morbid and hopeless philosophy that has sent so many of our youth into a search for other realities. Those who do not have hope, in an effort to drown their despair, turn to drugs or alcohol or other experiments that they think will break this stranglehold of futility. . . . This is the shattered visage of atheism. It has the stare of death, looking into the barren desert of emptiness and hopelessness.[6]

Exactly.

But it still doesn't explain "why." Why do atheists embrace this "stranglehold of futility," this "barren desert of emptiness and hopelessness"? Is it because, as Nietzsche claimed, atheism gives people strength?

That can't be true, since the most courageous men and women in history—the ones who sacrificed everything for some great cause—passionately believed in God.

Is it because atheism improves society?

That can't be true either, since we've already seen that the most significant contributions to human rights, civil rights, the arts, the sciences, and education were made by believers as well.

Is it because atheism builds character?

That certainly can't be true—because if this book has shown anything, it's that atheists are the most arrogant, ignorant, duplicitous, obnoxious, and ruthless bullies imaginable.

Is it because atheism is better equipped to alleviate the suffering of the world?

That is perhaps the most far-fetched theory of all. One quick glance at history is enough to see the vast amount of work done by religious people to help the poor, the sick, the mentally ill, the disabled, the elderly, and the dying. Even today, in a climate so saturated by the spirit of secularism, studies by ABC News, the Barna Group, and many other research organizations show that believers give four times the amount of time and money to charities as do atheists.[7]

Four times as much!

Indeed, when it comes to consoling the suffering, atheists seem intent on doing just the opposite.

When two parents tragically lose a child to cancer or some other disease and seek solace in the pages of the gospel, where they can read about Christ raising a little girl and a young man from the dead and saying: "I am the Resurrection and the Life . . . whoever believes in me will never die"[8]—these same heartbroken parents are told by writers like Dawkins and Harris that they are nothing more than dimwitted imbeciles who believe in fairy tales. The atheist message is: "Stop deluding yourself! You'll never see your child again. Get on with your life!"

When a stressed-out, beaten-down department store clerk wants to chase away the holiday blues by putting up a small Christmas tree and nativity scene, and by wishing harried shoppers a simple "Merry Christmas," the atheist police immediately pounce down upon him and squash his outrageous, intolerant message by threatening lawsuits. Like a chorus of grumpy Scrooges, they growl: "Every idiot who goes about with 'Merry

Christmas,' on his lips, should be boiled with his own pudding, and buried with a stake of holly through his heart."[9]

When an alcoholic or drug addict finally sees a glimmer of hope after so many years of living in darkness and despair, all because a twelve-step program convinced him to trust in a spiritual power greater than himself—the new atheists all scream with one voice: "There is no spiritual power greater than you, fool! There is no spiritual power at all!"

When a young man or woman feels called to give up worldly ambition in order to become a missionary in a foreign land or a pastor in the inner city or a friar working in a soup kitchen or a Sister cleaning the sores of lepers or a cloistered nun praying day and night for the world—when such selfless choices are made for the sake of God, atheists sneer in derision, and laugh: "Your sacrifice is a sham. Stop believing in myths! Go out and live for yourself, not for some make-believe deity!"

Yes, this is how atheists today demonstrate sympathy for those who are suffering.

"Oh, but it's not our job to console people," they retort. "All we care about is the truth."

The truth?

Please. The truth is that atheists have been engaged in a relentless campaign to distort the facts about history and theology and philosophy and religion for so long, they wouldn't recognize *the truth* if it stared them right in the face.

The truth is that no sane, sincere, and intelligent person could deny that there is a rational basis for believing in God. Though his existence cannot be proven scientifically, it can be shown logically and persuasively in dozens of ways. The truth is also that at the center of the atheist worldview is an absolutely unsolvable riddle:

Where did everything come from? Even atheists must concede that this ultimate question concerning the existence of the cosmos is shrouded in mystery—and must remain so forever.

That is the truth—the fair, honest, and objective truth.

If atheists, then, are in the dark about the deepest and most important realities of life—why are they so eager to destroy the solace that faith gives to so many people? Why do they insist on being so hateful and hostile, so callous and cold-blooded? If believing in God is able to offer even a drop of hope to those who are suffering so desperately, why are atheists so hell-bent on cruelly crushing that hope?

That is the *real* mystery we are dealing with.

From a purely psychological perspective, the answer may simply be that "misery loves company." Atheists believe in nothing, so they have no hope. This makes them nihilistic and negative, and therefore fundamentally unhappy. And like all negative and unhappy people, they want everyone else to be as unhappy as they are. They can't understand or accept it when other people don't share their hopeless outlook—and that makes them angry and resentful. The only way they can be content in their misery is to dismiss people of faith as being of lower intelligence than them. But even that is not enough to expunge the resentment they feel. So they spend their time doing their best to *deprive* others of their faith. "After all," they reason, "why should those religious simpletons be happy, any-way?" The final step in this thought process is to rationalize their hard-heartedness by citing all the "harm" that religion does to mankind. This bit of self-delusion conveniently puts atheists in the noble position of defending humanity—rather than kicking it when it is down.

In the end, the whole psychology of the militant atheist is both infantile and transparent.

Another plausible explanation for their hostility is that atheists desperately want to rid the world of any notion of transcendent truth—especially moral truth—because it stands in the way of their own decadent, selfish, and immoral desires. Peter Hitchens, in stark contrast to his atheist brother, Christopher, has made this argument many times in interviews and in his book, *The Rage Against God*.

To paraphrase his thinking: Why would anybody want to choose to believe in a totally chaotic, random universe—a gigantic cosmic car crash in which nothing had any significance beyond its immediate effect and your worldly life had no consequences after you were dead? The answer is so blazingly obvious it's barely worth asking the question: *atheists don't want those consequences; they don't want their actions to have any significance.* What they really want is unfettered hedonism. What they care about is themselves. Atheism is the worship of the self, and any belief system that contradicts the worship of the self—like Christianity—is a threat to them and their lifestyle.

But even with these explanations we still haven't solved the mystery of the unbelievers' unbridled ferocity. We haven't accounted for all the bloodshed, brutality, and butchery atheists have been responsible for these many years. That mystery is much more difficult to fathom, and solving it requires more than a mere understanding of psychology. Indeed, there is only one way to find the answer.

We have no choice but to embark on a path we have managed to avoid thus far in this book. We must indulge in speculation of a *spiritual* nature. We must look at this baffling enigma strictly from a believer's point of view—indeed, from a biblical point of view.

When we do that, everything finally begins to fall into place.

Bear in mind that what follows is derived mostly from revelation—from the revealed Word of God as it is found in Scripture and the tradition of the Christian church. It is not a philosophical argument, and it is not verifiable in any way. However, if we did not make this detour into the realm of theological conjecture, it would be impossible to discuss the atheist movement in its totality. It would be impossible to discover the *deepest* truth about the driving force behind it.

And the deepest truth is something very dark and very disturbing. We can get some hint of it by considering a few random words—words that for some strange reason keep appearing in the pages of this book—*pride, deception, murder, death,* and *suffering.*

We've used these words to describe the actions and characteristics of atheists over the course of the last few centuries, and especially over the last few years. But we need to take some time now to think about them more carefully. Where else have we seen these words strung together before? Where else have they appeared prominently in the annals of time?

To anyone who has read even a bit of Scripture, they have a ring of frightening familiarity; for these words, or variations of them, play an ominous role in both the first and last parts of the Bible—in the books of Genesis and Revelation. These two books—which are the object of particular scorn by atheists—focus on the very question we just alluded to—the question of the origin of existence.

Atheists mock these books because of all the allegorical

stories they tell: for instance, the story of God creating the world in six days and resting on the seventh, the story of Adam and Eve in the garden of Eden, the story of the Tree of the Knowledge of Good and Evil, the story of the serpent and the apple and the fall of man, the story of the war in heaven between Michael the Archangel and Satan.

Atheists love to say that these stories are silly myths, that they prove that Judaism and Christianity are bogus religions. But, as we've come to expect, when atheists attack the Bible and ridicule those who believe it, it's really just another example of their feeble attempt to tear down the faith with straw-man arguments. The majority of the faithful understand that these stories are meant as much more than factual accounts of historical events. Rather, they are theological allegories, laden with hidden meaning and symbolism. Their whole point is to convey profound and universal truths in a simple and poetic way— through the use of powerful metaphors and memorable images. That doesn't mean they aren't based on historical facts—or even that some of them aren't historically accurate—but that their primary message is theological in nature.

For example, the central meaning of the first chapter of the book of Genesis is not that God created the universe in six twenty-four-hour periods called days, but rather that the universe was indeed *created* out of nothing—and that it was *God* who did the creating. Moreover, God didn't haphazardly throw the cosmos together. He had a plan in mind from the beginning—a fixed and orderly plan.

We learn from attentive reading of this book that God—the "self-existing, noncontingent, uncaused cause" that philosophers have long speculated about—is not some philosophical abstraction, but rather a *personal* God: a God who purposely created the cosmos out of his goodness—specifically, out of his desire to share the goodness of existence with his creatures.

This is the essence of the biblical story of creation. And if atheists wish to ridicule it, they are the ones who demonstrate limited intellects because they are too shallow to see beyond the literal.[10]

But that's just the beginning of the truth revealed in Scripture. The first and last books of the Bible also pull back the veil that has covered the mystery of existence from time immemorial, showing us that when God created the universe he made much more than the planets and stars. He also created a whole spiritual world, full of pure spiritual beings called angels (about whom we'll talk more shortly).

And when God created humankind, he did not just make an animal composed of atoms and molecules, but fashioned a creature made in his image and likeness, a creature with a soul, an intellect, and free will.[11] In other words, he did not create a class of robots or computers, programmed to act in only one way; rather, he fathered a race of beings who are part physical and part spiritual and who have the ability to make their own decisions—to choose between good and evil.

The great biblical truth being conveyed is that the world *around us* and *within us* is not just material in nature but spiritual as well.

Scripture also tells us that the strange spiritual beings known as angels have free will too, and that when they were created a certain number of them chose to exercise that will *against* God. They chose to rebel against their Creator, to reject goodness, and to embrace evil instead. We don't know exactly what their motivation was, except that the sin of pride was involved and that the result of their insurrection was that the mutinous angels separated from God and doomed themselves forever to hell.[12]

How could anyone choose evil over good, hell over heaven? It's a tantalizing question, and decent people have trouble wrapping their minds around it. And yet, isn't it true that over and over again in the course of our own history, we've seen that it's possible to make such a choice? Haven't we seen crimes committed that are so abominable in nature that it curdles the blood to think about them? Consider all the atrocities we've discussed in this book—the mass murders, the tortures, the genocides, the infanticides. If the past has taught us anything at all, it's that spiritual pride and spiritual evil do exist; that it's possible not only to choose evil but to love it and hate all that is good.

That's why the story of the fall of the angels is so important. For believers, angels are not make-believe myths. They are *real* living beings. Christianity, Judaism, and Islam all proclaim their existence. These world religions teach not only that angels are pure spirits but that they have spectacular powers that are cosmic in magnitude, and that their number is prodigious. In fact, Scripture uses words such as *armies*, *legions*, and *multitudes* to describe them.[13]

So when a large segment of this multitude chose to rebel against God under the leadership of one angel in particular—whose name is known to us variously as Satan, Lucifer, and the Devil—it constituted an event of incredible significance that has ramifications for us even today.

Why?

Because having rebelled against the Creator, these so-called fallen angels, or demons, blame God for their miserable state. They hate him with all of their being and want nothing more than to lash out at him and hurt him in some way. That is the nature of spiritual pride. It breeds disobedience and hatred and a desire for revenge.

But there's a problem. How can anyone hurt God? How can anyone harm that which is all-powerful and invulnerable to any kind of conventional attack? It seems to be an impossible predicament.

There is really just one option. If you can't hurt God directly, your only course of action is to try to hurt that which bears the image of God. You try to hurt that which resembles God most, that which was made in God's likeness. In other words, you try to hurt those weak and wounded creatures known as human beings.

And that's exactly what the Devil and his demons have tried to do throughout history. From the moment the serpent tempted the first humans in the garden of Eden, dark spiritual forces have attempted to trick, deceive, injure, humiliate, mock, and murder human beings.

Their strategy has always been the same: to use deception to convince human beings to abuse their freedom, to make them believe that we can have all the power we want if only we disregard the will of God. The point of the story of the fall of man is not that Adam and Eve ate a real piece of fruit that was forbidden to them, but that human beings, at the instigation of the Devil, freely chose to turn away from God in prideful disobedience, in order to *make themselves into gods*. And as a result of that selfish decision, sin and suffering entered the world.

You see, when our first parents turned away from God, they turned away from everything that God is, and what they gained was not freedom or knowledge of any kind, but rather exposure to the harsh elements of a fallen world: death, decay, war, sickness, corruption, loneliness, old age, and the rest of the long catalog of human ills that have plagued humankind since time immemorial.

All of this came about as a result of the Devil's initiative. Yes, a *spiritual conflict* has been raging from the beginning of time, and the signs of it are still visible today. One only has to look at our all-pervasive culture of death to get some inkling of it. The Bible, for instance, says that God is the "Alpha and the Omega, the First and the Last, the Beginning and the End" (Rev. 22:13). But in the twenty-first century the Devil mocks God and says "No, *I* am the beginning and the end. Through abortion I control when human life begins, and through euthanasia I control when it ends." The Devil is always mocking God—always twisting and perverting what he says.

Even more chilling, have you even realized (as Father Frank Pavone has famously noted) that the same four words used by God to teach mankind the meaning of love are also used to promote the killing of unborn children?

"This is my body, which is given for you," Christ said to his disciples the night before he died.[14] He spoke these words in order to demonstrate how sacrificial love has the power to save the world and give life to others. But abortion supporters use the same expression to justify their pro-death views. "This is *my* body," they say. "I can do what I want with it, even to the point of killing the life within me."[15]

It's no accident that the same simple words are used for such different purposes—one to give life, the other to take life away. They are spoken from opposite ends of the universe and show that we are immersed in an age-old spiritual battle between life and death, truth and lies, humility and pride, good and evil.*

And what role do today's militant atheists play in this sinister struggle?

They are the proverbial Devil's pawns. Though they don't believe in the existence of either God or the Devil, they unwittingly act as diabolical instruments of spiritual evil—trumpeting secularism, hedonism, humanism, materialism, and moral relativism; fighting to advance euthanasia, abortion, infanticide, and the culture of death wherever possible and with all the resources at their command. Most importantly, they assist in the spiritual death of humanity. After all, though killing human beings is surely one of the Devil's greatest delights, nothing offends God more than the murder of immortal souls.

Consider the satanic strategy:

At the center of Christianity is the concept of *repentance*. Repentance simply means being sorry for sin; and being sorry for sin entails turning *away* from evil and *back* to God. Repentance thus represents a reversal of the sin of pride—a reversal of the original sin that was committed by the Devil and his demons, and by our first parents in the garden of Eden. It is an "undoing" of our rebellious nature and a sign of true faith. Christians believe that this "turning back to God" is an absolute prerequisite to entering heaven and achieving full union with God.

Christians also believe that God has made repentance easy

---

* This in no way implies that women who have had abortions are "evil." Indeed, most women who have abortions do so because they feel pressured by their doctors, boyfriends, husbands, families, friends, and by the whole culture of death. Most of these women are victims, and forgiveness and healing are always available to them.

for us. In fact, if you turn away from God by sinning, all you have to do is say that you're sorry and God will forgive you, no matter what the sin and no matter how many times you have committed it. We don't have time now to go into the whole theology of redemption, but the bottom line is that because of Christ's sacrifice on the cross, God has set the bar very low when it comes to forgiving our sins. Indeed, he has already done all the hard work of redemption for us. All we have to do is ask for forgiveness with sincerity—and he will grant it.** The heart of the Christian gospel is mercy.

The problem is, the Devil understands the concept of forgiveness too. He isn't stupid. He can read the Bible as well as anyone. So when he goes about the business of temptation, he's extremely aware that the person he's trying to lead away from God may thwart all his plans with a simple last-minute apology. Therefore his whole strategy must turn on something else—on an effort to ensure that the person he's tempting *doesn't repent in the first place.*

And this is where atheism comes in.

Atheism destroys the *very possibility* of repentance. After all, if you don't believe in God, there isn't anyone for you to apologize to, is there? Why say you're sorry for committing a sin when no one is even listening?

Similarly, atheism fosters an attitude of moral relativism. This is the ethical system we discussed several chapters ago. It basically says that because God doesn't exist, there is no such

---

** Different faith traditions have different ways of expressing repentance. For example, the Catholic church has an added Sacrament of Reconciliation.

thing as objective truth. Human beings are free to make their own rules and dispense with all biblical commandments.

This is, of course, the same lie spoken by the serpent in the garden of Eden, the same philosophy that seduced our first parents. It is Nietzsche's idea of the Superman all over again, and it is an extremely effective antidote against repentance. When human beings adopt moral relativism, there is no need for them to repent of their sins because they don't think they've committed any sins to begin with. They don't believe sin exists, so why apologize if there is nothing to apologize for?

And once more, the diabolical objective has been achieved.

In the final analysis, atheists act as accomplices to evil in three primary ways—first, by working to bring about the actual physical deaths of human beings; second, by creating an atmosphere of hopelessness that leads to despair and unhappiness in this life; and third, by strangling any impulse people have to faith and repentance, thereby destroying their hope for happiness in the next life.

They go about this malevolent work, for the most part, oblivious to the damage they're doing and the suffering they're causing. Indeed, atheists are oblivious to practically everything in life—to history, to philosophy, to theology, to psychology, to authentic science, to their own ruthlessness and the millions of corpses they've left in their wake. They're especially oblivious to the spiritual war that's being fought all around them—a war in which they are being used as demonic dupes. The most ironic thing of all is that, despite their profound state of ignorance, they actually think they are *more* intelligent than everyone else!

This is the desperate situation in which we find ourselves today. Truly evil forces are seeking our physical and spiritual destruction, and they are being aided and abetted by the most imbecilic fools on the planet!

There seems to be no hope.

And yet, there is one final point we haven't discussed; one final piece in this epic, tragic puzzle that may yet provide some encouragement to the beleaguered but stubborn individuals who still have the audacity to believe in God and to love him. What is it?

The next few pages will reveal the answer.

CHAPTER 10

THE END OF THE ATHEISTS

When Christopher Hitchens was diagnosed with terminal cancer in 2010, there was an outpouring of sympathy from believers around the world. Hitchens, the patron saint of the new atheist movement, was acerbic, combative, provocative, and often offensive in the extreme, but he could also be delightfully witty and likable. Many believers prayed for him during his illness and wrote encouraging letters to him. Hitchens took it all graciously, even commenting that the prayers were a show of concern, solidarity, and kindness. Nevertheless, he dismissed them as utterly useless and cited a 2006 study on the "Therapeutic Effects of Intercessory Prayer," in which no correlation could be found "between the number and regularity of prayers offered and the likelihood that the person being prayed for would have improved chances."[1]

This is typical of the kind of atheistic thinking that so confounds and frustrates people with common sense. It's one thing to say you don't believe in God—intelligent people can argue rationally about that. It's quite another to make a ridiculous attempt to empirically observe and measure how God might go about answering people who pray to him.

Aside from the preposterousness of the test variables (how in the world can you measure whether the prayers being "correlated" are sincere or not?), the whole premise of such an experiment is laughable. If there is a God, do atheists really think he's going to sit back and allow the puny creatures he made to cavalierly put him under a microscope and subject him to their little experiments—as if he were some kind of a high school science project? Would the all-powerful Creator of the universe really permit his creatures to treat him with the same condescending coldness they treat all the other material objects they handle?

Be serious! This is the same God who warned us: "You shall not put the LORD your God to the test."[2]

So the idea that prayer can be scientifically "disproved" is really just another silly example of scientism, the logical fallacy we spoke of several times already. The fact that Hitchens—a truly brilliant man—couldn't recognize this is more proof that the dogmatism of atheists is powerful enough to overwhelm their whole thinking process.

Ironically, in the last year of his life, Hitchens received a good deal of his care in a Catholic hospital in Washington DC with chaplains and nuns darting through the corridors, religious images on the walls, and crucifixes hung above all the doors— including the one in his room.

This interesting fact was reported by his wife in an interview she gave after his death, in which she complained that it was a bit "unsettling" to see such blatant Christian symbols all around them, especially while Hitchens lay on his bed, so sick. She said, "Perhaps we'd like to see a picture of the human genome. Perhaps that would be preferable to a giant Cross. I mean, how far is this going to get you in the modern world of medicine?"[3]

A human genome?

Even in the face of death, atheistic absurdity knows no limits. The purpose of the crosses on the walls, of course, was to serve as a reminder to all the sick and suffering patients in the hospital that God himself underwent great suffering too, and that no matter what the outcome of their particular ailment, the end of the human story is not death, but resurrection and life.

Predictably, atheists like Hitchens's wife failed to see either the simplicity or the sublimity of such a consoling message. Their intellectual shallowness is so profoundly deep that they immediately jumped to the conclusion that because a cross was hung on a hospital wall (instead of a genome), the hospital must therefore *not* value science and medicine as highly as it should.

Somehow they failed to notice the much more important (and obvious) fact that the hospital itself was Catholic. It wasn't an atheist hospital—there *are* none of those—and it wasn't even a privately owned secular hospital. It was a hospital founded by the church, built by the church, and administered, in large part, by the church.[4] Until the very end, the man who wrote that "religion poisons everything" couldn't escape religious kindness.

Of course atheists completely missed that gigantic irony. They were probably too busy worrying whether Hitchens might have a last-minute conversion. If their hero had done something as embarrassing as that, it would have been emotionally catastrophic for them. But as it turns out there was no need for concern. Hitchens remained a committed atheist to his last breath. His final whispered words were reportedly "capitalism" and "downfall."[5]

When these secular-sounding terms became public, atheists around the world gave a collective sigh of relief. They seemed to prove beyond any doubt that Hitchens had died an unbeliever. Once again, though, atheists missed the larger question: *Why were they worried in the first place?*

Could it be because so many atheists *do* turn back to God in their final years? After all, there have been many such unfortunate cases. In the last half of the twentieth century, the world's most famous unbeliever was an English philosopher named Antony Flew. Long before Dawkins, Dennett, Hitchens, and Harris attacked God and religion, Flew was the leading spokesman for the atheist movement.

An honorary member of the New Zealand Association of Rationalists and Humanists, and a fellow of the Committee for Skeptical Inquiry, Flew received many honors from the intellectual community, including the In Praise of Reason Award, in recognition of his "long-standing contributions to the use of methods of critical inquiry, scientific evidence, and reason in evaluating claims to knowledge and solving social problems."[6]

Then, in 2004, the unthinkable happened. Flew shocked the world by announcing he had come to believe in God. His defection threw atheists into a frenzy. They immediately turned on him and began to question whether his conversion might be due to his declining mental capacities.[7]

Flew, however, remained sharp as a whip. When asked why he had become a believer, he calmly replied:

There were two factors in particular that were decisive. One was my growing empathy with the insight of Einstein and other noted scientists that there had to be an Intelligence behind the integrated complexity of the physical Universe. The second was my own insight that the integrated complexity of life itself—which is far more complex than the physical Universe—can only be explained in terms of an Intelligent Source. I believe that the origin of life and reproduction simply cannot be explained from a biological standpoint despite numerous efforts to do so. With every passing year, the more that was discovered about the richness and inherent intelligence of life, the less it seemed likely that a chemical soup could magically generate the genetic code. The difference between life and non-life, it became apparent to me, was ontological and not chemical. The best confirmation of this radical gulf is Richard Dawkins' comical effort to argue in The God Delusion that the origin of life can be attributed to a "lucky chance." If that's the best argument you have, then the game is over. No, I did not hear a Voice. It was the evidence itself that led me to this conclusion.[8]

Doesn't sound much like "declining mental capacities," does it? Nevertheless, atheists unleashed a storm of invective against Flew (that's what they do best), and to this day they are licking their wounds. Hence their anxiety over a possible Hitchens conversion.

The bottom line is that the longer an atheist lives, the greater the chances that he or she will begin to see the illogic and inconsistency of the atheist position. There's a certain amount of wisdom that's acquired as one gains more experience in life—and wisdom is the enemy of falsehood.

Added to this is another even more compelling reason why atheists have a natural tendency to become believers as they grow older. And it doesn't have anything to do with science, philosophy, or even the fear of death. It has to do with something called the "dead-end rule."

This rule simply says that if you go down a dead-end street and either ignore or don't see the sign that says it's a dead end, you will soon learn by *personal experience* that the road comes to an end.

It doesn't matter if you're convinced the sign is wrong or if you like the road you're traveling on better than the other roads you see; disregarding the sign will lead you to a place you don't want to go, a place with no outlet, a place, perhaps, of great danger—such as a steep cliff. And the only way to escape is to turn around and go back the way you came.

All through its history, the church has been putting up dead-end signs along the road to atheism. Many people have chosen to ignore those signs, especially in recent times, but that doesn't change the truth of the signs' message. Individuals who proclaim themselves to be atheists, or who lead functionally atheistic lives, eventually learn by painful experience that atheism is a dead end.

We've said this many times in this book, but it bears repeating: Human beings have a natural, inborn yearning for the transcendent; a deep desire for goodness, love, and eternity—a thirst for God. When Christ said in the gospel of John that only God has the power to give us "living water," and that whoever drinks this water "will never be thirsty again," that's what he was talking about.[9]

Whether they know it or not, atheists, too, are searching for "living water" that can satisfy their thirst for God. When they delete God from their lives, a dry, arid vacuum is left in their souls that needs to be filled. Atheists do their best to fill it with many things: money, work, power, sex, scholarship, fitness, pleasures, distractions, scientism, stoicism, pantheism, and hedonism. Mostly they try to fill the void up with *themselves*. Instead of worshipping God, they become their own deity, their own idol.

Only none of these things works. None of them has the power to fill the God-void. None can help atheists make sense of all the suffering and tragedy in the world. None can provide them with even the smallest ray of hope, the tiniest bit of consolation. None can satiate their thirst for the transcendent.

In the end, atheism doesn't have the "stuff" that happiness is made of. Human beings simply cannot survive without hope, and atheism is the philosophy of hopelessness. That's why it's been such an utter failure throughout history. Just try naming one societal ill that atheism has ever solved. You can't—because there aren't any. On the other hand, there's no end to the misery it has caused.

So while many embrace atheism at first, and are even content for a while, they eventually learn for themselves how devastatingly bleak, black, and hopeless the path of unbelief is. And when they get to the end of the road, they either make the choice to go over the cliff, like Christopher Hitchens, or turn back, like Antony Flew.

More people than ever before, it seems, are making the choice to jump over the precipice and into the abyss. But no force in the world can ever make the majority of human beings lose their common sense or their desire for happiness. No matter how many atheist books are written, no matter how many atheist celebrities curse the church, no matter how many laws restricting religious freedom are passed by the government, it's impossible to abolish the impulse to believe in God. You might as well try to abolish human nature itself. The great mass of humanity will always turn around when they reach the precipice and come back. And when they return—healed of their hopelessness—they become new dead-end signs for everyone else to see.

The truth is, atheism, as a belief system, is on a collision course with itself. Despite the arrogance of the new atheists, the facts speak for themselves: The atheist movement as a whole is shrinking globally. According to an extensive study undertaken by the Pew Research Center, by the year 2050, the number of atheists, agnostics, and religiously unaffiliated, "though increasing in countries such as the United States and France . . . will make up a declining share of the world's total population."[10]

The study reports that the Christian population of the earth is expected to be an incredible *2.9 billion* by the middle of the twenty-first century, with the number of Muslims not far behind.[11] The reason for this explosion is that, in recent years, Christianity has been growing at an extraordinary rate in Latin America, Africa, and Asia.[12]

In Africa, for instance, there were only 8.7 million Christians in 1900; there are now 390 million, and by 2025 the number is expected to be 600 million.[13] Likewise, Asia's Christian population, which is presently 350 million, is projected to grow to 460 million in that same time period.[14]

Most interestingly, the number of Chinese Christians has

also skyrocketed. While there were only four million in 1949, there are now sixty-seven million.[15] Bear in mind, the People's Republic of China is still a Communist country whose official government religion is atheism. Though religious freedoms have improved, for most of the twentieth century Chinese religious institutions were under strict government control, and many religious practices were banned outright. Yet Christianity is now growing there, constituting 5 percent of the population as of 2007.[16]

The same is true for Russia. Under the Communist regime of the Soviet Union, religion had been banned and persecuted for seventy years, and there had been a truly brutal program of forced conversion to atheism. The official objective of the state was the elimination of all existing religions and the prevention of future religious belief through the indoctrination of the young. In spite of this comprehensive plan—carried out with ruthless efficiency for seven decades—there are almost one hundred million Christians living in Russia today, and estimates are that figure will double by 2050.[17]

The bottom line is that people can be forced, coerced, indoctrinated, or persecuted into accepting atheism, but eventually they rebel; eventually they go back to believing. Faith is like a steel rubber band, eternally elastic, forever returning to its true form. Atheism, on the other hand, doesn't have the inherent capability of living very long—because in truth, it is dead already.

The question is, how long will it take for atheism in the West to collapse under its own weight? Or, if you prefer, how long will it take for the snake to devour itself?

And that's where believers can play a crucial role. Indeed,

believers in the twenty-first century have an important choice to make. They can either delay the end of atheism or hasten its demise.

In the final analysis, the only reason atheism exists today and is thriving in the United States and Europe is because believers allow it to. Believers make atheism possible. Not the true believers—not the ones who walk the walk and make the necessary sacrifices; not the ones whose belief is reflected in their behavior—but rather, the ones who "play" at believing; the ones for whom God has little or no relevance in life; the ones who reject the very dogmas they're supposed to hold fast to.

These are the so-called "Cafeteria Christians" who pick and choose the tenets of faith that are easiest to follow and most pleasing to them personally; the ones who end up promoting values just as secular as the secular culture in which they live. In other words, these are the functional atheists we've talked so much about. It is because of the prevalence of hypocrites such as these that the new atheism has flourished in recent decades, and its hopeless, death-centered agenda has been able to advance so far.

If these believers practiced what they professed to believe, the fruits of their faith would be so abundant that atheism could never gain any kind of foothold in society. It simply wouldn't be able to take root and grow. It would be crowded out and suffocated, as it has at other times in history. In the presence of truth, error always flees. In the presence of good, evil always dies—eventually.

Today's functional atheists have been the great enablers of unbelief. They've given unbelievers so much breathing space and nourishment that it's been possible for them to increase their ranks to an unprecedented degree, and as a result, atheism has spread like a plague to every segment of Western society.

Something similar can be said about those who identify themselves as agnostic.

These indecisive, wishy-washy, modern-day Hamlets may not know it, but they, too, are enablers; they, too, are functional atheists. The agnostic position attempts to get around the responsibility—and the obligation—of making a choice about God. The agnostic says: "I'm not against believing, but I'm just not sure. You'll have to prove it to me first. If you prove it, then I'll believe."[18]

The only problem with this kind of thinking is that it goes against everything the Judeo-Christian God stands for. The personal God of the Old and New Testaments is all about freedom. Of course, he could make a huge, blazing cross appear in the sky, and then everyone would have no option but to believe in his existence. But he doesn't want to force us to do anything.

Instead, he gives us all the evidence we need to make a free choice—all the evidence of nature and logic and common sense and reliable testimonies and revelation. Then he leaves it up to us to decide. That's why faith is not, ultimately, a feeling, but rather a decision: an informed, intelligent decision, but a decision nonetheless. The fact is, nothing you do or read in your life will ever give you anything resembling a mathematical proof that either God exists or doesn't exist. It always comes back to the necessity of making a choice. You *must* make a choice.

That's the point agnostics miss. They think they can just sail through life without making a real decision about God and it won't cost them anything. But that's self-delusion. It *does* cost them something. It costs them their identity as believers; it costs them the grace and transformational power that comes as a result of having that identity. It costs them hope, without which there can be no romance or adventure or freedom. Most of all, it costs them their relationship with God—a relationship that could be the source of indescribable joy, both in this life and the next.

We've been so brainwashed by secularists into believing that the greatest thing in the world to have is an open mind, and the greatest thing to do is to search for answers. But that's nonsense. The whole point of searching for something is to eventually find it. The whole point of having an open mind is so that it can eventually close—on the truth. An open mind is not an amorphous mind. A worthwhile search is not an endless one. If you're past thirty years old and haven't made a definitive decision about God, then your priorities are screwed up. You're deluding yourself about what you actually are—a functional atheist, an enabler of unbelief. You can't afford to waste any more time. It's time to get off the fence!

Ultimately, the tragedy of Christopher Hitchens's life is not that he died too soon, but that he failed in his search to find the truth. He failed to find it even when it was staring him right in the face.

As he lay on his hospital bed, weak and suffering, I'm sure he looked up at least occasionally and saw that big cross hanging over the doorway. That great, central symbol of Christianity contained all the truth he could ever hope for.

It contained the truth that there *is* a God and that he is not merely some abstraction but a personal, caring Creator and Father. It contained the truth that he is a Father who loves us so much that he became one of us and even suffered death for us in order to make up for the sin of our first parents in the garden of

Eden. It contained the truth that the key to life is love; the key to love is self-sacrifice; and the key to self-sacrifice is the surrender of our own will in order to do the will of the Father.

It contained the truth about the mystery of evil in the world. Hitchens spent his whole life battling what he considered to be evils—political evils, economic evils, social evils. But the greatest evil ever committed was right there over his hospital door—the evil of the crucifixion.

This was, without question, the single most appalling act of ingratitude, deception, betrayal, depravity, obscenity, and malevolence of all time. God—the Creator of everything and everyone—was killed by his own creatures. The crime was not simply homicide or patricide or fratricide or even genocide. It was deicide. No evil in the universe could ever come close to the crucifixion and death of Christ.

Yet what did God manage to do with the most monstrous of all human deeds?

Out of the darkness of the crucifixion he brought forth the light of the resurrection. In a stunning and miraculous act of reversal, God turned evil on its head—redeeming mankind, elevating the human person to a divine level, making it possible for sins to be forgiven and for us to receive countless blessings during our earthly lifetime. On top of this he threw open the gates of heaven so that one day we could all be reunited with our friends and loved ones in an eternity of happiness.

In dying for us, God didn't bring just a little good out of evil. He was somehow able to bring the greatest good out of the greatest evil. No more horrible event could have taken place than the killing of Christ. No more wonderful gift could have been given to humanity than the resurrection.

And if God was able to turn the worst kind of evil into the greatest kind of good, doesn't that also mean that he can turn lesser kinds of evils into good as well? Doesn't that mean he can take the bad things that happen to us in our lives and somehow transform them and bring some kind of blessing out of them? This is the truth about the mystery of suffering. This is the truth about the resurrection. And this is the truth that was contained in the cross hanging over Hitchens's hospital door.

Atheists need to take note of that truth, because it has direct bearing on their goal to eradicate God and religion from the face of the earth. It's a truth that applies in a special way to the church Christ founded—a church that has somehow managed, over the course of two thousand years, to resist all efforts to destroy it.

In his great book *The Everlasting Man*, G. K. Chesterton wrote the following words—words that the militant atheists of the twenty-first century should consider carefully:

> Europe has been turned upside down over and over again; and at the end of each of these revolutions the same religion has again been found on top. The Faith is always converting the age, not as an old religion but as a new religion. . . . At least five times, with the Arian and the Albigensian, with the Humanist skeptic, after Voltaire and after Darwin, the Faith has to all appearance gone to the dogs. In each of these five cases it was the dog that died. . . . It was supposed to have been withered up at last in the dry light of the Age of Reason; it was supposed to have disappeared ultimately in the earthquake of the Age of Revolution. . . . Science explained it away; and it was still there. History disinterred it in the past; and it appeared suddenly in the future. Today it stands

once more in our path; and even as we watch it, it grows. . . .
Christianity has died many times and risen again; for it had a
God who knew the way out of the grave.[19]

Had Christopher Hitchens meditated longer on the cross
hanging in his hospital room, he might have seen this truth. He
might have seen that his own death could even be considered
a metaphor for it. He was, after all, the brightest, wittiest, and
most formidable proponent of the new atheist movement. And
yet, today he is gone; but the faith, as ever, remains.

"Heaven and earth will pass away," Christ said, "but my
words will not pass away."[20]

The civilization of antiquity, the civilization of the Middle
Ages, the civilization of the Renaissance, the civilization of the
Enlightenment, the civilization of the Industrial Revolution,
the civilization of the early modern world—all these great and
magnificent civilizations have come and gone. Even now, our
own secular, space-age, techno civilization is flying fast before
our eyes, and will soon disappear into dust. And still those words
of Christ have not passed away.

That is because they are the truth—and the truth always
goes on. It outlasts lies, blasphemies, and enemies, no matter
how formidable. You can hide it, persecute it, denigrate it, scoff
at it, lock it up, even murder it—but all to no avail. Christopher
Hitchens tried his best to escape from it, but his efforts were
futile. Just as he couldn't get away from the fact that he was
born with the very name of God branded into his identity—
Christopher, after all, means "bearer of Christ"—so, too, he
couldn't get away from the cross of Christ as he lay dying.

In the end, God always has the last word. No matter who

or what the adversary, he always wins; for he always brings order out of chaos, light out of darkness, faith out of faithlessness, happiness out of misery, hope out of despair, victory out of defeat, life out of death, good out of evil.

God is so powerful he can somehow bring good out of absolutely anything . . .

Yes, even out of the atheists.

SUGGESTED READING

Adler, Mortimer J. *How to Prove There Is a God: Mortimer J. Adler's Writings and Thoughts About God*. Edited by Ken Dzugan. Chicago: Open Court, 2011.

Adler, Mortimer J. *How to Think About God*: *A Guide for the 20th-Century Pagan*. New York: Touchstone, 1991.

Adler, Mortimer J. *Six Great Ideas*. New York: Touchstone, 1997.

Aquinas, Thomas. *Summa Contra Gentiles, Book One: God*. Translated by Anton C. Pegis. Notre Dame, IN: University of Notre Dame Press, 1975.

Aquinas, Thomas. *Summa Contra Gentiles, Book Two: Creation*. Translated by James F. Anderson. Notre Dame, IN: University of Notre Dame Press, 1975.

Aquinas, Thomas. *Summa Contra Gentiles, Book Three: Providence*. Translated by Vernon J. Bourke. Notre Dame, IN: University of Notre Dame Press, 1976.

Aquinas, Thomas. *Summa Contra Gentiles, Book Four: Salvation*. Translated by Charles J. O'Neil. Notre Dame, IN: University of Notre Dame Press, 1975.

Aquinas, Thomas. *Summa Theologica I–V.* Translated by the Blackfriars. Edited by Thomas Gilby. New York: Image Books, 1969.

Aristotle. *The Metaphysics.* Translated by John H. McMahon. Mineola, NY: Dover, 2007.

Augustine. *Confessions.* Edited by Michael P. Foley. Translated by F. J. Sheed. Indianapolis: Hackett Publishing Company, 2006.

Augustine. *The City of God Against the Pagans.* Edited and translated by R. W. Dyson, Cambridge: Cambridge University Press, 1998.

Berger, Peter. *A Rumor of Angels: Modern Society and the Rediscovery of the Supernatural.* New York: Doubleday, 1969.

Berlinski, David. *The Devil's Delusion: Atheism and Its Scientific Pretensions.* New York: Basic Books, 2009.

Buckley Jr., William F. *God and Man at Yale: The Superstitions of "Academic Freedom."* Washington DC: Regnery Publishing, 2002.

Buckley Jr., William F. *Nearer, My God: An Autobiography of Faith.* New York: Doubleday, 1997.

Bugliosi, Vincent. *Divinity of Doubt: The God Question.* New York: Vanguard Press, 2011.

Chesterton, G. K. *Orthodoxy.* New York: Image Books, 2001.

Chesterton, G. K. *St. Thomas Aquinas.* San Francisco: Ignatius Press, 2002.

Chesterton, G. K. *The Autobiography of G. K. Chesterton.* San Francisco: Ignatius Press, 2006.

Chesterton, G. K. *The Everlasting Man.* New York: Dover Publications, 2012.

Clark, Ronald W. *Einstein: The Life and Times*. New York: Avon Books, 1984.

Collins, Francis S. *The Language of God: A Scientist Presents Evidence for Belief*. New York: Free Press, 2006.

Dante. *Paradiso*. Translated by Robert Hollander and Jean Hollander. New York: Anchor Books, 2008.

Dante. *Purgatorio*. Translated by Jean Hollander and Robert Hollander. New York: Anchor Books, 2004.

Dante. *The Inferno*. Translated by Robert Hollander and Jean Hollander. New York: Anchor Books, 2002.

Day, Vox. *The Irrational Atheist: Dissecting the Unholy Trinity of Dawkins, Harris, and Hitchens*. Dallas: Benbella Books, 2008.

DeStefano, Anthony. *Angels All Around Us: A Sightseeing Guide to the Invisible World*. New York: Image, 2011.

DeStefano, Anthony. *Ten Prayers God Always Says Yes To: Divine Answers to Life's Most Difficult Problems*. New York: Doubleday, 2007.

D'Souza, Dinesh. *What's So Great About Christianity*. Washington DC: Regnery Publishing, 2007.

Eagleton, Terry. *Reason, Faith, and Revolution: Reflections on the God Debate*. New Haven: Yale University Press, 2009.

Farrell, John. *The Day Without Yesterday: Lemaître, Einstein, and the Birth of Modern Cosmology*. New York: Thunder's Mouth Press, 2005.

Ferris, Timothy. *The Whole Shebang: A State-of-the-Universe(s) Report*. New York: Touchstone, 1998.

Feser, Edward. *The Last Superstition: A Refutation of the New Atheism*. South Bend, IN: St. Augustine's Press, 2008.

Geisler, Norman L. and Frank Turek. *I Don't Have Enough Faith to Be an Atheist*. Wheaton, IL: Crossway Books, 2004.

Greene, Brian. *The Elegant Universe: Superstrings, Hidden Dimensions, and the Quest for the Ultimate Theory*. New York: W. W. Norton, 2003.

Greene, Brian. *The Fabric of the Cosmos: Space, Time, and the Texture of Reality*. New York: Vintage Books, 2005.

Hague, William. *William Wilberforce: The Life of the Great Anti-Slave Trade Campaigner*. Orlando: Harcourt, 2007.

Hahn, Scott, and Benajmin Wiker. *Answering the New Atheism: Dismantling Dawkins' Case Against God*. Steubenville, OH: Emmaus Road Publishing, 2008.

Hawking, Stephen. *A Brief History of Time*. New York: Bantam Books, 1988.

Hitchens, Peter. *The Rage Against God: How Atheism Led Me to Faith*. New York: HarperCollins, 2010.

Horn, Trent. *Answering Atheism: How to Make the Case for God with Logic and Clarity*. El Cajon, CA: Catholic Answers Press, 2013.

Johnson, Phillip E., and John Mark Reynolds. *Against All Gods: What's Right and Wrong About the New Atheism*. Downers Grove, IL: InterVarsity Press, 2010.

Kamen, Henry. *The Spanish Inquisition: A Historical Revision*. New Haven: Yale University Press, 2014.

Keller, Timothy. *Counterfeit Gods: The Empty Promises of Money, Sex, and Power, and the Only Hope That Matters*. New York: Dutton, 2009.

Keller, Timothy. *The Reason for God: Belief in an Age of Skepticism*. New York: Dutton, 2008.

Kempis, Thomas À. *The Imitation of Christ.* Uhrichsville, OH: Barbour Publishing, 2013.

Kumar, Manjit. *Quantum: Einstein, Bohr and the Great Debate About the Nature of Reality.* New York: W. W. Norton, 2011.

Lennox, John C. *God and Stephen Hawking: Whose Design Is It Anyway?* Oxford: Lion Hudson, 2011.

Lennox, John C. *Gunning for God: Why the New Atheists Are Missing the Target.* Oxford: Lion Hudson, 2011.

Levin, Mark. *Men in Black: How the Supreme Court Is Destroying America.* Washington DC: Regnery Publishing, 2006.

Lewis, C. S. *Mere Christianity.* New York: HarperOne, 2001.

Lewis, C. S. *Miracles.* New York: HarperOne, 2001.

Lewis, C. S. *The Four Loves.* New York: Harcourt, 1971.

Lewis, C. S. *The Problem of Pain.* New York: HarperOne, 2001.

Lewis, C. S. *The Screwtape Letters.* New York: HarperOne, 2001.

Limbaugh, David. *Jesus on Trial: A Lawyer Affirms the Truth of the Gospel.* Washington DC: Regnery Publishing, 2014.

Livio, Mario. *Brilliant Blunders: From Darwin to Einstein— Colossal Mistakes by Great Scientists That Changed Our Understanding of Life and the Universe.* New York: Simon & Schuster, 2013.

McGrath, Alister. *The Dawkins Delusion? Atheist Fundamentalism and the Denial of the Divine.* Downer's Grove, IL: InterVarsity Press, 2010.

McGrath, Alister. *Twilight of Atheism: The Rise and Fall of Disbelief in the Modern World.* Oxford: Oxford University Press, 2004.

Merton, Thomas. *The Seven Storey Mountain*. Orlando: Harcourt, 1998.

O'Donnell, James J. *Augustine Confessions II: Commentary on Books 1–7*. Oxford: Oxford University Press, 2012.

O'Donnell, James J. *Augustine Confessions III: Commentary on Books 8–13*. Oxford: Oxford University Press, 2012.

Panek, Richard. *The 4% Universe: Dark Matter, Dark Energy, and the Race to Discover the Rest of Reality*. New York: Mariner Books, 2011.

Peters, Edward. *Inquisition*. Berkeley: University of California Press, 1989.

Poole, Michael. *The 'New' Atheism: 10 Arguments That Don't Hold Water?* Oxford: Lion Hudson, 2009.

Rummel, R. J. *Death by Government*. New Brunswick, NJ: Transaction Publishers, 1994.

Scott, Otto. *Robespierre: The Fool as Revolutionary; Inside the French Revolution*. New York: Mason and Lipscomb Publishers, 1974.

Strobel, Lee. *The Case for Christ: A Journalist's Personal Investigation of the Evidence for Jesus*. Grand Rapids: Zondervan, 1998.

Susskind, Leonard. *The Black Hole War: My Battle with Stephen Hawking to Make the World Safe for Quantum Mechanics*. New York: Little, Brown, 2008.

Turek, Frank. *Stealing from God: Why Atheists Need God to Make Their Case*. Colorado Springs: NavPress, 2014.

Woods, Thomas E. *How the Catholic Church Built Civilization*. Washington DC: Regnery Publishing, 2012.

Vost, Kevin. *From Atheism to Catholicism: How Scientists Led Me to Truth*. Huntington, IN: Our Sunday Visitor, 2010.

Zacharias, Ravi. *The Real Face of Atheism.* Grand Rapids: Baker
    Books, 2009.

BIBLES

The Holy Bible, New International Version. Grand Rapids:
Zondervan, 1984.

The Holy Bible, Revised Standard Version Catholic Edition. San
    Francisco: Ignatius Press, 1994.

The Holy Bible, King James Version. Grand Rapids: Zondervan,
2010.

ACKNOWLEDGMENTS

I would like to express my gratitude to all the good people at Thomas Nelson, especially Brigitta Nortker, Stephanie Tresner, Sara Broun, and my brilliant editor, Webster Younce, who has helped me in so many different ways and is the person most responsible for the publication of this book.

I would also like to thank my literary manager of fifteen years, Peter Miller; my colleague and best friend, Jerry Horn; my gifted research assistant, Jonathan Caulk; my personal assistant, the wonderful Danielle Malina-Jones; and the great man to whom this book is dedicated, Father Frank Pavone, national director of Priests for Life.

Finally, I want to thank the most important person in my life—my wise, good, beautiful, and loving wife, Jordan.

ABOUT THE AUTHOR

Anthony DeStefano is the bestselling author of more than fifteen Christian books for adults and children. He has hosted two television series on EWTN and has received many awards and honors from religious organizations throughout the world. A Knight of the Sovereign Military Order of Malta, he is an avid pilot, a successful businessman, and a longtime pro-life activist. He lives with his wife, Jordan, in New Jersey.

NOTES

Chapter 1: The Arrogance of the Atheists

1. "Responding to Arrogant Children," Nobullying.com, last modified December 22, 2015, https://nobullying.com /arrogant/.

2. Friedrich Nietzsche, "The Parable of the Madman," in *Thus Spoke Zarathustra: A Book for All and None*, trans. Walter Kaufmann (Princeton: Princeton University Press, 2013); "Now that the Nietzsche Archive is open, the question is finally also open as to whether and how eastern Germans will confront the Nazification of Neitzsche. . . . Might eastern Germans begin to face the past by facing Nietzsche? It will be hard indeed to confront the last century of German intellectual history without addressing him. . . . In July 1934, Hitler and reigning Nazi ideologue Alfred Rosenberg visited [Neitzsche's sister] Elisabeth and presented her with a wreath for her brother's grave bearing the word 'To a Great Fighter.'" John Rodden, *Repainting the Little Red Schoolhouse: A History of Eastern German Education, 1945–1995* (New York: Oxford University Press, 2002), 288–89; Thomas Mann, a German novelist, contemporary of

Nietzsche, and the 1929 Nobel Laureate winner wrote that Nietzsche "served the Germans as a model for those traits which made them a disaster and a terror to the world, and led them ultimately to ruin themselves: romantic passion; will which is free because it has no goal and aspires to the infinite." Thomas Mann, "Nietzsche's Philosophy in the Light of Recent History," in *Last Essays*, trans. Richard and Clara Winston and Tania and James Stern (New York: Knopf, 1959), 175. Quoted in Mark W. Clark, *Beyond Catastrophe: German Intellectuals and Cultural Renewal After World War II, 1945–1995* (Oxford: Lexington Books, 2006), 112.

3. Sam Harris, *Letter to a Christian Nation* (New York: Vintage Books, 2008), 67, 51.

4. Remarks come from a speech Richard Dawkins presented at the Edinburgh International Science Festival on April 15, 1992. Quoted in Alec Fisher, *The Logic of Real Arguments*, 2nd ed. (Cambridge: Cambridge University Press, 2004), 83.

5. Bill Maher, *Religulous*, directed by Larry Charles (2008; Santa Monica, CA: Lionsgate, 2009), DVD.

6. Christopher Hitchens, *God Is Not Great: How Religion Poisons Everything* (New York: Twelve Books, 2007), 64.

7. "Now, our statement is this—that the Deity is an animal that is everlasting and most excellent in nature; so that with the Deity life and duration are uninterrupted and eternal: for this constitutes the very essence of God." Aristotle, *The Metaphysics*, trans. John H. McMahon (Mineola, NY: Dover, 2007), 277.

8. *Stanford Encyclopedia of Philosophy*, s.v. "Francis Bacon," https://plato.stanford.edu/entries/francis-bacon.

9. Francis Bacon, "Theological Tracts," *The Works of Francis Bacon, Lord Chancellor of England*, vol. 2 (Philadelphia: Carey and Hart, 1841), 405.

10. Leonardo da Vinci's own words: "That man becomes happy who follows Christ." *The Notebooks of Leonardo Da Vinci*, vol. 1, trans. Edward MacCurdy (New York: George Braziller, 1955), 86.

11. "Godliness consists in the knowledge love & worship of God, Humanity in love, righteousness & good offices towards man." Isaac Newton, "A Short Schem of the True Religion," The Newton Project, February 2002, http://www.newtonproject. ox.ac.uk/view/texts/normalized/THEM00007.

12. "While both religion and natural science require a belief in God for their activities, to the former He is the starting point, to the latter the goal of every thought process." Max Planck, *Scientific Autobiography and Other Papers*, trans. Frank Gaynor (New York: Philosophical Library, 1949), 184; "The dance of atoms, electrons, and nuclei, which in all its fury is subject to God's eternal laws, has been entangled with another restless universe which may well be the Devil's: the human struggle for power and domination, which eventually becomes history." Max Born, *The Restless Universe*, trans. Winifred M. Deans (New York: Dover Publications, 2012), 279. Daniel Bernoulli was raised a Protestant Christian. His father, Johann, wrote in his autobiography that his parents "spared no trouble or expense to give me a proper education in both morals and religion. This religion was the Calvinist faith which had forced his grandparents to flee from Antwerp to avoid religious persecution." J. J. O'Connor and E. F. Robertson, "Johann Bernoulli," School of Mathematics and Statistics, University of St. Andrews, accessed March 30, 2017, http://www-history.mcs. st-andrews.ac.uk/Biographies/Bernoulli_Johann.html.

13. "To know the mighty works of God, to comprehend His wisdom and majesty and power; to appreciate, in degree, the wonderful working of His laws, surely all this must be a pleasing and acceptable mode of worship to the Most High, to whom ignorance cannot be more grateful than knowledge." Copernicus, quoted in Francis S. Collins, *The Language of God: A Scientist Presents Evidence for Belief* (New York: Free Press, 2006), 230–31; "I suppose the parts of the universe to be in the best arrangement, so that none is out of its place, which is to say

that Nature and God have perfectly arranged their structure." Galileo, quoted in Stillman Drake, "Galileo Galilei to Francesco Ingoli," *Galileo at Work: His Scientific Biography* (Mineola, NY: Dover Publications, 2003), 294; "I feel carried away and possessed by an unutterable rapture over the divine spectacle of heavenly harmony. . . . I cast the die and write a book for the present time, or for posterity. It is all the same to me. It may wait a hundred years for its readers, as God also has waited six thousand years for an onlooker." Kepler, quoted in Max Caspar, *Kepler,* trans. and ed. C. Doris Hellman (New York: Dover Publications, 1993), 267.

14. In addition to being a botanist, Otto Brunfels was a Carthusian monk whose "*Pandectarum Veteris et Noui Testamenti,* one of the first Protestant biblical concordances, was first published in 1527, became very influential, and was reprinted several times in subsequent years." Gergely M. Juhász, *Translating Resurrection: The Debate Between William Tyndale and George Joye in Its Historical and Theological Context*, ed. Robert J. Bast (Leiden, Netherlands: Koninklijke Brill, 2014), 241; William Turner was influenced by the preaching of Hugh Latimer, was chaplain to the duke of Somerset, and published a "small religious book, 'Unio Dissidentium,' in 1538." *Dictionary of National Biography 1885–1900*, vol. 57, ed. Sidney Lee (New York: Macmillan, 1899), 363; Herman Boerhaave's belief in God in the words of Samuel Johnson: "He was an admirable example of temperance, fortitude, humility, and devotion. His piety, and a religious sense of his dependence on God, was the basis of all his virtues, and the principle of his whole conduct." Samuel Johnson, *The Works of Samuel Johnson, LL.D.,* vol. 2, 3rd ed. (New York: Alexander V. Blake, 1846), 313.

15. Biographer Édouard Grimaux notes how Lavoisier's faith in God didn't waver in the face of his impending execution in 1794 during the French Revolution: "Raised in a pious family which had given many priests to the Church, he had held to

his beliefs." Charles McKenna, "Antoine-Laurent Lavoisier," *The Catholic Encyclopedia,* vol. 9 (New York: Robert Appleton Company, 1910), http://www.newadvent.org/cathen/09052a .htm.

16. "I do not understand how anyone can doubt the sincerity and constancy of my attachment to the religion which I profess, the Roman, Catholic and Apostolic religion in which I was born and brought up. . . . In this faith I recognise a pure gift of God, a supernatural grace." Alessandro Volta on faith, quoted in Karl Alois Kneller, *Christianity and the Leaders of Modern Science: A Contribution to the History of Culture in the Nineteenth Century,* trans. T. M. Kettle (London: B. Herder, 1911), 117; "On the day of his wife's death [Ampère] wrote two verses from the Psalms, and the prayer, 'O Lord, God of Mercy, unite me in Heaven with those whom you have permitted me to love on earth.'" William Fox, "André Marie Ampère," *The Catholic Encyclopedia,* vol. 1 (New York: Robert Appleton Company, 1907), http ://www.newadvent.org/cathen/01437c.htm.

17. "Faraday solemnly vowed to live according to the precepts laid down in the Bible and in imitation of Christ's perfect example." Geoffrey Cantor, *Michael Faraday: Sandemanian and Scientist: A Study of Science and Religion in the Nineteenth Century* (London: Macmillan Press, 1991), 5.

18. "Posterity will one day laugh at the foolishness of the modern materialistic philosophers. The more I study nature, the more I stand amazed at the works of the Creator. I pray while I am engaged in my work in the laboratory." Pasteur, quoted in "Is Darwinism on Its Death-bed?" *Sanitarian* 50, no. 398 (1903): 242.

19. Albrecht von Haller, a well-known figure in Europe in his day, treasured his time in his hometown of Bern, Switzerland, where he remained an obscure figure, writing in a letter to a friend: "I can serve God here with all my strength." Charles Bert Reed, *Albrecht von Haller: A Physician—Not Without Honor*

(Chicago: Chicago Literary Club, 1915), 48; "[William] Harvey is often hailed as a modern who helped to free the world from the shackles of superstitious allegiance to scholasticism and Christianity. . . . But on closer inspection this view cannot stand. Take for example the following passage from his *Exercises*: 'We acknowledge God, the supreme and omnipotent creator, to be present in the production of all animals, and to point, as it were, with a finger to his existence in his works' (Exercise 54). By shedding light on the works of nature, Harvey saw himself as illuminating God's handiwork." Brian T. Kelly, "Illuminating God's Handiwork: Why We Study William Harvey," Thomas Aquinas College, April 1, 2016, https://thomasaquinas.edu/news /illuminating-gods-handiwork-why-we-study-william-harvey.

20. William Keen said in his 1922 commencement address for Crozer Theological Seminary: "Sage and wayfaring man alike find in it guidance and comfort in this mortal life, and the Gospel, the good news of an Immortal Life through our Lord Jesus Christ." William Keen, *I Believe in God and Evolution* (Philadelphia: J. B. Lippincott Company, 1922), 20; Joseph Murray asked, "Is the Church inimical to science? Growing up as a Catholic and a scientist—I don't see it. One truth is revealed truth, the other is scientific truth. If you really believe that creation is good, there can be no harm in studying science." Quoted in Christopher Kaczor, "The Church Opposes Science: The Myth of Catholic Irrationality," Catholic Education Resource Center, 2012, http://www.catholiceducation.org/en /science/catholic-contributions/the-church-opposes-science -the-myth-of-catholic-irrationality.html.

21. "My experiences with science led me to God. They challenge science to prove the existence of God. But must we really light a candle to see the sun?" Werhner von Braun to the California State Board of Education, September 14, 1972, quoted in Christopher H. K. Persaud, *Blessings, Miracles & Supernatural Experiences: A Biblical Perspective; A Christian's Story* (Colorado

Springs: Standard Publishing Company, 1925); "[Walton] argued that there was a continuous revelation of God through science in probing the wonders of nature and the original act of creation and, 'we must pay God the compliment of studying his work of art.'" Vincent McBrierty, "Ernest Thomas Sinton Walton: Nobel Laureate" (Memorial Discourse, Dublin, Ireland, April 16, 2012), https://www.tcd.ie/Secretary/ FellowsScholars /discourses/discourses/2012_V%20McBrierty%20on%20ETS %20Walton.pdf; "The more I work with the forces of Nature and sense the Divine good-will towards mankind the more I am brought into contact with the great truth: that everything is ordered by the Lord and Giver of Life and this so-called science I work with is just an expression of the Supreme Will which wants to put human beings in contact with each other to help them improve and have a greater mutual understanding." Guglielmo Marconi to Maria Cristina Marconi, March 9, 1927, in Maria Cristina Marconi, *Marconi My Beloved*, ed. Elettra Marconi (Boston: Dante University of America Press, 2001), 30; "I may now state, as the result of a long life spent in studying the *works* of the Creator, that I am satisfied they afford far more satisfactory and more convincing proofs of the existence of a supreme Being than any evidence transmitted through human testimony can possibly supply." Charles Babbage, *Passages from the Life of a Philosopher* (London: Longman, Green, Longman, Roberts, & Green, 1864), 403.

22. "Those who have obtained the farthest insight into Nature have been, in all ages, firm believers in God." William Whewell, quoted in Charles Noel Douglas, *Forty Thousand Quotations, Prose and Poetical* (London: George G. Harrap, 1917), 681.

23. "I cannot anyhow be contented to view this wonderful universe, and especially the nature of man, and to conclude that everything is the result of brute force. I am inclined to look at everything as resulting from designed laws, with the details,

whether good or bad, left to the working out of what we may call chance. Not that this notion *at all* satisfies me." Charles Darwin, *The Life and Letters of Charles Darwin,* vol. 2, ed. Francis Darwin (New York: D. Appleton, 1896), 104.

24. Lemaître's theory was at first rejected by Einstein and the scientific establishment. "While Einstein was not biased against Lemaître's religious background, he did call the priest's physics 'abominable.' . . . However, in 1929 Einstein was forced to eat humble pie. Edwin Hubble, working at Mount Wilson Observatory in Southern California, showed that all the distant galaxies in the universe were racing away from one another as though they were debris from a cosmic explosion. The Big Bang model seemed to be correct." Simon Singh, "Even Einstein Had His Off Days," *New York Times,* January 2, 2005, http://www.nytimes.com/2005/01/02/opinion/even-einstein -had-his-off-days.html?_r=0; Mark Midbon, "'A Day Without Yesterday': Georges Lemaitre & the Big Bang," Catholic Education Resource Center, March 2000, http ://www.catholiceducation.org/en/science/faith-and-science /a-day-without-yesterday-georges-lemaitre-amp-the-big -bang.html.

25. G. K. Chesterton, "The Man in the Cave," in *The Everlasting Man* (Radford, VA: Wilder Publications, 2008), 6.

26. Joel Primack quoted in Stefan Lovgren, "Evolution and Religion Can Coexist, Scientists Say," *National Geographic News,* October 18, 2004, http://news.nationalgeographic.com /news/2004/10/1018_041018_science_religion.html.

27. George Sylvester Viereck, *Glimpses of the Great* (New York: Macaulay Company, 1930), 372–73.

28. Prince Hubertus of Lowenstein claims Einstein said this before World War II. Quoted in Ronald W. Clark, *Einstein: The Life and Times* (New York: Avon Books, 1984), 516.

29. Philipp A. Frank, *Einstein: His Life and Times,* trans. George Rosen, ed. Shuichi Kusaka (New York: Da Capo Press, 1947), 284.

Chapter 2: The Ignorance of the Atheists

1. Theodore Gray, "For That Healthy Glow, Drink Radiation!" *Popular Science*, August 17, 2004, http://www.popsci.com /scitech/article/2004-08/healthy-glow-drink-radiation.

2. In the United States, working-class women were hired to decorate wristwatch faces with radium paint. Rebecca Hersher, "Mae Keane, One of the Last 'Radium Girls,' Dies at 107," *All Things Considered*, National Public Radio, December 28, 2014, http://www.npr.org/2014/12/28/373510029/ saved-by-a-bad-taste-one-of-the-last-radium-girls-dies-at-107.

3. "When Elton Met Jake," *Guardian*, November 12, 2006, https ://www.theguardian.com/music/2006/nov/12/popandrock9.

4. Adam Rathe, "Gwyneth Paltrow Decides to Raise Kids Apple and Moses as Jewish—Despite Not Believing in Religion." *New York Daily News*, July 21, 2011, http://www .nydailynews.com/entertainment/gossip/gwyneth-paltrow -decides-raise-kids-apple-moses-jewish-not-believing -religion-article-1.160057.

5. Ron Steelman, "Bill Murray Philosopher/Humanist?," *Steelman the Humanist* (blog), December 2, 2012, https ://steelmanthehumanist.com/2012/12/02/bill-murray -philosopher-humanist/. This quote has been widely attributed to Murray in articles going back as far as 2012, but the original source cannot be located. A 2016 Snopes report did attempt to debunk the quote, but was not convincing. Murray, meanwhile, has not issued any disclaimers.

6. Bill Maher, *Religulous*, directed by Larry Charles (2008; Santa Monica, CA: Lionsgate, 2009), DVD.

7. John H. Richardson, "Larry Flynt: What I've Learned," *Esquire*, January 29, 2007, http://www.esquire.com/news-politics /interviews/a1646/larry-flynt-interview-0399.

8. Richard Dawkins, *The God Delusion* (New York: Mariner Books, 2008), 51.

9. "It is misleading to think or speak of Greek institutions of

higher learning—even the major Athenian philosophical schools—as 'universities' in the medieval or modern sense. . . . Neither the teachers of the schools nor the schools themselves were licensed or certified, nor were formal examinations given or degrees awarded to those who completed their studies. Even though many of the schools used public property, they were entirely private organizations, self-regulating and self-supporting." John Patrick Lynch, *Aristotle's School: A Study of a Greek Educational Institution* (Berkeley: University of California Press, 1972), 66; Old Roman education "reflected the practical and simple virtues of a farming people oriented around family and community." And after a thousand years of development in early antiquity, "late ancient schools still probably corresponded more closely to private, guild-like associations of the earlier Greek and Roman days than to the chartered universities that appeared in the High Middle Ages." George Thomas Kurian and Mark A. Lamport, eds., *Encyclopedia of Christian Education* (Lanham, MD: Rowman & Littlefield, 2015), 45, 47.

10. "The university is a European institution; indeed, it is the European institution *par excellence.* . . . As a community of teachers, accorded certain rights, such as administrative autonomy and the determination and realization of curricula (courses of study) and of the objectives of research as well as the award of publicly recognized degrees, it is a creation of medieval Europe, which was the Europe of papal Christianity." Walter Rüegg, "foreword," to *A History of the University in Europe, Volume 1: Universities in the Middle Ages*, eds. Walter Rüegg and H. De Ridder-Symoens (Cambridge: Cambridge University Press, 1992), xix.

11. "Illuminating a Dark Age," *Economist*, December 16, 2010, http://www.economist.com/node/17722535.

12. *The Routledge International Encyclopedia of Education*, eds. Gary McCulloch and David Crook (New York: Routledge, 2008), s.v. "compulsory education."

13. Jack Huberman, *The Quotable Atheist: Ammunition for Nonbelievers, Political Junkies, Gadflies, and Those Generally Hell-Bound* (New York: Nation Books, 2007), vii.

14. Rob Boston, "The Art of Censorship," *Church and State*, Americans United for Separation of Church and State, January 2011, https://www.au.org/church-state/ january-2011-church-state/featured/the-art-of-censorship.

15. "So, what *does* it mean to be created in God's image? The Hebrew root of the Latin phrase for image of God—*imago Dei*—means image, shadow or likeness of God. You are a snapshot or facsimile of God. At the very least this means humans occupy a higher place in the created order because we alone are imprinted with godlike characteristics." Dick Staub, "What 'Made in the Image of God' Really Means," *Relevant*, March 4, 2013, http://www.relevantmagazine.com/god/ deeper-walk/features/23549-qmade-in-the-image-of-godq (link no longer accessible).

16. From a translated letter of a Roman citizen that reveals the fate of unwanted baby girls: "Hilarion to Alis his sister, heartiest greetings, and to my dear Berous and Apollonarion. Know that we are still even now in Alexandria. Do not worry if when all the others return I remain in Alexandria. I beg and beseech of you to take care of the little child, and as soon as we receive wages I will send them to you. If—good luck to you!—you bear offspring, if it is a male, let it live; if it is a female, expose it." Quoted in *Selections from the Greek Papyri*, ed. and trans. George Milligan (Cambridge: Cambridge University Press, 1910), 32–33.

17. "In Europe, infanticide tended to involve abandonment and exposure, while in China exposure and drowning predominated. . . . Usually the newborn girl was drowned by the mother or a midwife in a bucket of water kept beside the birth bed." D. E. Mungello, *The Great Encounter of China and the West, 1500–1800*, 4th ed. (Lanham, MD: Rowman & Littlefield, 2013), 144, 148.

18. "In its many forms, death in the arena was public, official, and communicative; and, when properly conducted, spectacles of death were comforting and entertaining for Romans of all classes. Spectacles played a major role in the festival calendar, the social life, and the public space of ancient Rome for over a millennium. With industry and pride, Rome scoured the Empire for victims, built monumental facilities, orchestrated events, and immortalized these performances in art, architecture, and literature." Donald G. Kyle, *Spectacles of Death in Ancient Rome* (London: Routledge, 1998), 2–3.

19. "Only someone who is religious can speak seriously of the sacred. . . . We may say that all human beings are inestimably precious, that they are ends in themselves, that they are owed unconditional respect, that they possess inalienable rights, and, of course, that they possess inalienable dignity. In my judgment these are ways of trying to say what we feel a need to say when we are estranged from the conceptual resources [i.e. God] we need to say it. . . . Not one of [these statements about human beings] has the power of the religious way of speaking . . . that we are sacred because God loves us, his children." Raimond Gaita, quoted in Timothy Keller, *The Reason for God: Belief in an Age of Skepticism* (New York: Dutton, 2008), 154.

20. Dinesh D'Souza, *What's So Great About Christianity* (Washington DC: Regnery Publishing, 2007), 77.

21. "The Bible begins with an explicit affirmation that marriage is between one man and one woman (Gen 1–2), an affirmation which is later confirmed by Jesus himself (Matt 19:4–6). . . . And then, in the New Testament, Paul's command to Timothy that church leaders must be, alongside exemplars of other moral virtues, 'the husband of one wife' (1 Tim 3:2, 12; cf. 1 Tim 5:9) implies that polygamy is not a desirable thing." Lionel Windsor, "Polygamy in the Bible: A Sordid Tale," *The Briefing*, Matthias Media, June 13, 2012, http://matthiasmedia.com /briefing/2012/06/polygamy-in-the-bible-a-sordid-tale.

22. Thomas A. J. McGinn discusses the forced prostitution of slaves and the lack of slaves' legal standing in *Prostitution, Sexuality, and the Law in Ancient Rome* (Oxford: Oxford University Press, 1998), 56; see also *Ancient Greek Democracy: Readings and Sources,* ed. Eric W. Robinson (Malden, MA: Blackwell Publishing, 2004).

23. "We have clear evidence, however, that women were included as full members of early Christian communities. For example, Saul (before his conversion) sets out to arrest both men and women who had adopted the new faith of Christianity (Acts 8:3; 9:2)." Barbara J. MacHaffie, *Her Story: Women in Christian Tradition*, 2nd ed. (Minneapolis: Fortress Press, 2006), 3.

24. For more on women in the early church, see Catherine Kroeger, "The Neglected History of Women in the Early Church," *Christian History*, no. 17 (1988), https ://www.christianhistoryinstitute.org/magazine/article/ women-in-the-early-church.

25. For more on the Christian view of slavery, see Lee Strobel, *The Case for Christ* (Grand Rapids: Zondervan, 1998).

26. The early Christian church thrived as an egalitarian alternative to the exclusive religious institutions of the Roman Empire. "[Roman] religion excluded slaves from its functions, which, it was held, their presence would have defiled. (Cicero, 'Octavius', xxiv). Absolute religious equality, as proclaimed by Christianity, was therefore a novelty. The Church made no account of the social condition of the faithful. Bond and free received the same sacraments. Clerics of servile origin were numerous (St. Jerome, Ep. lxxxii). The very Chair of St. Peter was occupied by men who had been slaves—Pius in the second century, Callistus in the third." Paul Allard, "Slavery and Christianity," *The Catholic Encyclopedia*, vol. 14 (New York: Robert Appleton Company, 1912), http://www.newadvent. org/cathen/14036a.htm.

27. Wilberforce on the African slave trade: "So enormous, so

dreadful, so irremediable did its wickedness appear that my own mind was completely made up for the abolition. . . . Let the consequences be what they would, I from this time determined that I would never rest until I had effected its Abolition." William Hague, *William Wilberforce: The Life of the Great Anti-Slave Trade Campaigner* (Orlando: Harcourt, 2007), 141.

28. "During the 1830s, the majority of abolitionists were Northern white churchgoers and their clergy. . . . The mode of conversion to abolitionism was identical with the revival style of worship. The process began with the penitent's initial conviction of personal sin of having been proslavery, followed by expressions of heartfelt repentance, and pledges to follow the divine command that all human kind were equal in God's sight." Bertram Wyatt-Brown, "American Abolitionism and Religion," National Humanities Center, http://nationalhumanitiescenter. org/tserve/nineteen/nkeyinfo/amabrel.htm.

29. "One fact which, in the Church, relieved the condition of the slave was the absence among Christians of the ancient scorn of labour. . . . Converts to the new religion knew that Jesus had been a carpenter; they saw St. Paul exercise the occupation of a tentmaker (Acts 18:3; 1 Corinthians 4:12). 'Neither did we eat any man's bread', said the Apostle, 'for nothing, but in labour and in toil we worked night and day, lest we should be chargeable to any of you' (2 Thessalonians 3:8; cf. Acts 20:33, 34)." Paul Allard, "Slavery and Christianity," *The Catholic Encyclopedia*, vol. 14 (New York: Robert Appleton Company, 1912), http://www.newadvent.org/cathen/14036a.htm.

30. Frank Lambert thoroughly examines the religious affiliations and beliefs of the Founding Fathers in his book *The Founding Fathers and the Place of Religion in America* (Princeton: Princeton University Press, 2003).

31. Ari Ben-Menahem, *Historical Encyclopedia of Natural and Mathematical Sciences,* vol. 1 (Berlin: Springer, 2009), 424.

Chapter 3: The Ruthlessness of the Atheists

1. "Joseph Goebbels: Chief of Nazi Propaganda," Holocaust Online, accessed July 28, 2017, http://holocaustonline.org /joseph-goebbels/.

2. Charles Phillips and Alan Axelrod, eds., *Encyclopedia of Wars* (New York: Facts on File, 2005).

3. R. J. Rummel, *Death by Government* (New Brunswick, NJ: Transaction Publishers, 1994), 9.

4. Ibid., 8.

5. Stéphane Courtois, et al., *The Black Book of Communism: Crimes, Terror, Repression*, trans. Jonathan Murphy and Mark Kramer, ed. Mark Kramer (Cambridge: Harvard University Press, 1999), 4.

6. Beale (under his penname Vox Day) is quoted by Ken Ammi in "Atheism," Creation Ministries International, June 18, 2009, http://creation.mobi/atheism#atheism-communism.

7. "Atheists waged a 70-year war on religious belief in the Soviet Union. The Communist Party destroyed churches, mosques, and temples; it executed religious leaders; it flooded the schools and media with anti-religious propaganda; and it introduced a belief system called 'scientific atheism,' complete with atheist rituals, proselytizers, and a promise of worldly salvation." Paul Froese, "Forced Secularization in Soviet Russia: Why an Atheistic Monopoly Failed," *Journal for the Scientific Study of Religion* 43, no. 1 (2004): 35; for more on the brutal methods Stalin employed to repress Christians, see "The Clergy" chapter in Alexander N. Yakovlev's *A Century of Violence in Soviet Russia* (New Haven: Yale University Press, 2002), 153–68.

8. For an in-depth history on Stalin's purges and terror tactics, see Robert W. Thurston, *Life and Terror in Stalin's Russia: 1934–1941* (New Haven: Yale University Press, 1996).

9. The victims of the brutal man-made famine imposed by Stalin's regime in 1932–1933 are memorialized and honored at http ://www.holodomorct.org/.

10. For an in-depth study on murder during Stalin's regime and throughout the lifespan of the Soviet Union, see R. J. Rummel, *Lethal Politics: Soviet Genocide and Mass Murder Since 1917* (New Brunswick, NJ: Transaction Publishers, 1996).

11. "Of a total of 2,720 clergy recorded as imprisoned at Dachau, some 2,579 (or 94.88%) were Catholic and a total of 1,034 clergy were recorded overall as dying in the camp, with 132 'transferred or liquidated' during that time—although R. Schnabel's 1966 investigation found an alternative total of 2,771, with 692 noted as deceased and 336 sent out on 'invalid trainloads' and therefore presumed dead." Paul Berben, *Dachau 1933–1945: The Official History* (London: Norfolk Press, 1975), 276–77.

12. H. R. Trevor-Roper, ed., *Hitler's Table Talk: 1941–1944*, trans. Norman Cameron and R. H. Stevens (New York: Enigma Books, 2007), 8.

13. Ibid., 7.

14. Ibid., 60.

15. Ibid., 111.

16. Ibid., 260.

17. Steve Weidenkopf, "Were the Crusades Just Wars?" *Catholic Answers*, November 4, 2014, https://www.catholic.com /magazine/online-edition/were-the-crusades-just-wars.

18. For further reading on the Christian response to the Muslim invasion, see Steve Weidenkopf, *The Glory of the Crusades* (El Cajon, CA: Catholic Answers Press, 2014).

19. "It is clear that for most of its existence the Inquisition was far from being a monster of death either in intention or in capability. . . . It would seem that during the sixteenth and seventeenth centuries fewer than three people a year were executed by the Inquisition in the whole of the Spanish monarchy from Sicily to Peru, certainly a lower rate than in any provincial court of justice in Spain or anywhere else in Europe." Henry Kamen, *The Spanish Inquisition: A Historical Revision*, 4th ed. (New Haven: Yale University Press, 2014), 254.

20. Dave Armstrong cites the work of eminent non-Catholic historians (including Kamen) who agree the death toll has been greatly exaggerated. He quotes Edward Peters, a professor at the University of Pennsylvania, who states: "The best estimate is that around 3000 death sentences were carried out in Spain by Inquisitorial verdict between 1550 and 1800, a far smaller number than that in comparable secular courts." Dave Armstrong, "Were '50-68 Million' Killed in the Inquisition?" *Biblical Evidence for Catholicism* (blog), Patheos, August 21, 2015, http://www.patheos.com/blogs/davearmstrong/2015/08/50–68-million-killed-in-the-inquisition.html.

21. John Shertzer Hittell, *A Brief History of Culture* (New York: D. Appleton, 1875), 137.

Chapter 4: The Intolerance of the Atheists

1. Jerry Coyne, "Keith Kloor Lumps Me with Dawkins as Sneering, Strident, and Simplistic," *Why Evolution Is True* (blog), December 28, 2012, https://whyevolutionistrue.wordpress.com/2012/12/28/keith-kloor-lumps-me-with-dawkins-as-sneering-strident-and-simplistic/.

2. Sam Harris quoted in Bethany Saltman, "The Temple of Reason: Sam Harris on How Religion Puts the World at Risk," *Sun*, September 2006, http://thesunmagazine.org/issues/369/the_temple_of_reason.

3. Sam Harris, *The End of Faith: Religion, Terror, and the Future of Reason* (New York: W. W. Norton, 2004), 52–53.

4. Bill Maher on *Jimmy Kimmel Live*, ABC, January 7, 2015, https://archive.org/details/WPVI_20150108_043500_Jimmy_Kimmel_Live.

5. "The Four Horseman–Hitchens, Dawkins, Dennet, Harris [2007]," YouTube video, 1:57:14, posted by "CaNANDian," July 23, 2012, https://www.youtube.com/watch?v=n7IHU28aR2E.

6. "Christopher Hitchens—Religion," YouTube video, 8:36, from a debate at the University of Toronto in November 2006, posted by "BlissfulKnowledge," March 14, 2007, https://www.youtube .com/watch?v=PY8fjFKAC5k.

7. Al Stefanelli, "Taking the Gloves Off . . . When Diplomacy Fails, It's Time to Fight Using the Law," American Atheists, September 14, 2011, http://str.typepad.com/files /americanatheists_eradicatethechristians.pdf.

8. Richard Dawkins, quoted in Gary Wolf, "The Church of the Non-Believers," *Wired*, November 1, 2016, https://www.wired .com/2006/11/atheism.

9. Sam Harris, "Science Must Destroy Religion," *Huffington Post*, January 2, 2006, updated May 25, 2011, http://www .huffingtonpost.com/sam-harris/science-must-destroy-reli_b_13153.html.

10. Nicholas Humphrey, "What Shall We Tell the Children?" *Edge*, February 21, 1997, https://www.edge.org/conversation /nicholas_humphrey-what-shall-we-tell-the-children.

11. Giovanni Santostasi, quoted in Zoltan Istvan, "Some Atheists and Transhumanists Are Asking: Should It Be Illegal to Indoctrinate Kids with Religion?" *Huffington Post*, September 15, 2014, http://www.huffingtonpost.com/zoltan-istvan/some -atheists-and-transhu_b_5814484.html.

12. Ibid.

13. John Laurence von Mosheim, *Institutes of Ecclesiastical History, Ancient and Modern: Volume I.—Primitive Period*, trans. James Murdock (London: Longman, Brown, Green and Longmans, 1850), 72.

14. G. K. Chesterton, *The Everlasting Man* (Mineola, NY: Dover Publications, 2012), 161.

15. "It would have no Christ, no Mohammed. . . . The new religion would have festivals, a large number of them. They would be named in honor of the Human Race, Liberty, Equality, Agriculture and Industry, Posterity and other noble

revolutionary subjects." Otto Scott, *Robespierre: The Voice of Virtue* (New Brunswick, NJ: Transaction Publishers, 2011), 224.

16. "Anybody could join in smashing images, vandalizing churches (the very word was coined to describe this outburst of iconoclasm), and theft of vestments to wear in blasphemous mock ceremonies. Those needing pretexts could preach national necessity when they tore down bells or walked off with plate that could be recast into guns or coinage. . . . The Parisian detachments marching to Lyons left a trail of pillaged and closed churches, and smoldering bonfires of ornaments, vestments, and holy pictures all along their route." William Doyle, *The Oxford History of the French Revolution*, 2nd ed. (Oxford: Oxford University Press, 2002), 260–61.

17. Scott, *Robespierre*, 108.

18. "The total number of death sentences during the Terror (including Paris) was 16,594. But many more people died without formal death sentences imposed in a court of law. Many perished in overcrowded and unsanitary prisons while awaiting trial. . . . A classic study of the statistics of the Terror was made by the American historian Greer who estimated an overall total of 41,000 victims. . . . More realistic estimates, such as that by Jean-Clément Martin, suggest up to 250,000 insurgents and 200,000 republicans met their deaths in a war in which both sides suffered appalling atrocities." Marisa Linton, "The Terror in the French Revolution," Kingston University, http://www .port.ac.uk/special/france1815to2003/chapter1/interviews /filetodownload,20545,en.pdf.

19. Michael R. Lynn, "Executions, the Guillotine and the French Revolution," The Ultimate History Project, http://www .ultimatehistoryproject.com/executions-the-guillotine-and-the -french-revolution.html.

20. Ruth Scurr, *Fatal Purity: Robespierre and the French Revolution* (New York: Owl Books, 2006), 305.

21. "Atheists: Nobody Needs Christ at Christmas," American

Atheists, December 3, 2013, http://news.atheists.org/2013/12 /03/press-release-atheists-nobody-needs-christ-at-christmas/.

22. Thaddeus M. Baklinski, "Most Americans Want to Hear 'Merry Christmas,'" Catholic Online, December 15, 2009, http://www .catholic.org/news/hf/faith/story.php?id=35028.

23. Thomas Jefferson, *Notes on the State of Virginia*, ed. William Peden (Chapel Hill: University of North Carolina Press, 1982), 159.

24. Mark R. Levin, *Men in Black: How the Supreme Court Is Destroying America* (Washington DC: Regnery Publishing, 2005), 53.

Chapter 5: The Shallowness of the Atheists

1. Vincent Bugliosi, *Divinity of Doubt: The God Question* (New York: Vanguard Press, 2011), 41.

2. Vincent Bugliosi, "Why Do I Doubt Both the Atheists and the Theists?" *Huffington Post*, April 12, 2011, http://www .huffingtonpost.com/vincent-bugliosi/why-do-i-doubt-both -the-a_b_844611.html.

3. "Deep Misunderstanding About the Bible by Fr. Robert Barron," YouTube video, 7:35, posted by "Resource777," March 25, 2013, https://www.youtube.com /watch?v=htxOjJHB5-8.

4. G. K. Chesterton, *All Things Considered* (New York: John Lane Company, 1909), 277–78.

5. The late evolutionary biologist (and atheist) Stephen Jay Gould defined evolution without mentioning origin: "*Evolution* is a process of continuous branching and diversification from common trunks. This pattern of irreversible separation gives life's history its basic directionality." *Merriam-Webster*, s.v. "evolution," https://www.merriam-webster.com/dictionary /evolution.

6. Michael Poole, *The 'New' Atheism: Ten Arguments That Don't Hold Water?* (Oxford: Lion Hudson, 2009), 49–50.

7. In a 2007 debate with Richard Dawkins at the Oxford Museum

of Natural History, "Has Science Buried God?," mathematician John Lennox observed that "when Newton discovered the law of gravity he didn't say 'Marvelous, now I know how it works; I don't need God," "Lennox Vs. Dawkins Debate—Has Science Buried God?," YouTube video, 1:20:36, posted by "ThickShades0," June 18, 2011, https://www.youtube.com /watch?v=J0UIbd0eLxw.

Chapter 6: The Cowardice of the Atheists

1. Christopher Hitchens, *The Missionary Position: Mother Teresa in Theory and Practice* (New York: Twelve Books, 2012).
2. Hitchens signed on with Aroup Chatterjee to smear Mother Teresa's reputation in a documentary, hatefully titled *Hell's Angels*. "Although Hitchens did none of the research, he took command of the project as if he had. . . . He also presented the documentary to the public as if it had been his idea all along. . . . According to Chatterjee, he lied when he said that he edited the film and was involved in the post shooting." Bill Donohue, *Unmasking Mother Teresa's Critics* (Manchester, NH: Sophia Institute Press, 2016), 12.
3. "The Vatican takes the cause of sainthood seriously. With regard to Mother Teresa, the inquiry [concerning her possible sainthood] collected thirty-five thousand pages of documentation and testimony and interviewed many witnesses; the probe took two years to complete. The investigation also established a twelve-member episcopal team, known as devil's advocates, whose purpose was to challenge the claims of those lobbying for sainthood. Even Mother Teresa's most notorious critic, Christopher Hitchens, was summoned for testimony." Ibid., 4; Christopher Hitchens, "Mommie Dearest: The Pope Beatifies Mother Teresa, a Fanatic, a Fundamentalist, and a Fraud," *Slate*, October 20, 2003, http://www.slate.com/articles /news_and_politics/fighting_words/2003/10/mommie _dearest.html.

4. Preston Ni, "The Truth About Bullies and How to Deal with Them," *Psychology Today*, January 8, 2014, https://www .psychologytoday.com/blog/communication-success/201401 /the-truth-about-bullies-and-how-deal-them.

5. Maher has criticized Islam in the media and on his HBO show *Real Time with Bill Maher*. Sam Harris has criticized Islamic fundamentalism publicly and in his books and articles, including *The End of Faith: Religion, Terror, and the Future of Reason* (New York: W. W. Norton, 2004). Richard Dawkins has criticized Islam publicly and in his writing. For his critique of Islam in the context of the Danish cartoon drawings of Muhammad in the mid-2000s, see *The God Delusion* (New York: Mariner Books, 2008), 46–49.

6. Anti-theists—Proactive Atheists Opposing Religious Harm. 2013. "If Mary Had Had an Abortion, We Wouldn't Be in this Mess." Facebook, March 23, 2013, https://www.facebook.com /RichardDawkinsFoundation/posts/121583994698241. This same group has also created a tee-shirt with this statement that atheists can proudly wear: https://www.zazzle.com/antitheist _if_mary_had_had_an_abortion_shirt-235445808725274271.

7. Ken Ammi, "Atheism—The New (Emergent) Atheists, part 4 of 4," *True Free Thinker* (blog), http://www.truefreethinker.com /articles/atheism-new-emergent-atheists-part-4-4.

8. Penny Starr, "Atheist: 'Okay for Those on the Left to Critique, Mock, Deride Christianity, but Islam Gets a Free Pass,'" CNS News, October 30, 2015, http://www.cnsnews.com/news/ article/penny-starr /atheist-okay-disparage-christians-islam-limits-because-fear.

9. Ibid.

10. Friedrich Nietzsche, *The Complete Works of Friedrich Nietzsche: Volume Twelve: Beyond Good and Evil,* ed. Oscar Levy (New York: MacMillan, 1914), 59, 61, 228.

11. "Christopher Hitchens About His Book 'God Is Not Great at Google,'" YouTube video, 1:06:32, posted by "NonBeliever

Archive," August 8, 2015, https://www.youtube.com
/watch?v=WYH2fvED674.

12. Barry Arrington, "The New Atheists Are Simpering Cowards,"
    Uncommon Descent (blog), February 7, 2015, http://www.
    uncommondescent.com/intelligent-design/the-new-atheists
    -are-simpering-cowards/.

13. Ibid.

14. "Bishop Barron on Atheists at the CNN Belief Blog," YouTube
    video, 8:06, posted by "Bishop Robert Barron," June 28, 2011,
    https://www.youtube.com/watch?v=OOJjI5Yv5TU.

15. "Bishop Barron on the New Atheists," YouTube video, 7:00,
    posted by "Bishop Robert Barron," February 18, 2009, https
    ://www.youtube.com/watch?v=Xe5kVw9JsYI.

16. "He himself is the fuel our spirits were designed to burn, or the
    food our spirits were designed to feed on." C. S. Lewis, *Mere
    Christianity* (New York: HarperOne, 2001), 50.

17. Augustine, *Confessions*, ed. Michael P. Foley, trans. F. J. Sheed
    (Indianapolis: Hackett Publishing Company, 2006), 3.

18. "This world in itself is not reasonable, that is all that can be said.
    But what is absurd is the confrontation of this irrational and the
    wild longing for clarity whose call echoes in the human heart."
    Albert Camus, *The Myth of Sisyphus, and Other Essays*, trans.
    Justin O'Brien (New York: Vintage, 1991), 21.

Chapter 7: The Death-Centeredness of the Atheists

1. John 10:10 NABRE.

2. Proverbs 8:36.

3. Philip Kuchar, "The Culture of Atheism," *The Secular Web*,
   June 17, 2007, https://infidels.org/kiosk/article/the-culture
   -of-atheism-759.html.

4. Conservative commentator Patrick J. Buchanan on America's
   movement toward secularism in the 1960s and beyond: "This
   revolution involved the repudiation of America's past as racist,
   sexist, imperialist, and genocidal. . . . This revolution involved

the rejection and overthrow of traditional Christian morality and Christianity itself as bigoted and repressive, and the conversion of the young to a sensuality, self indulgence, and promiscuity condemned by all Christian faiths. This revolution involved the overturning of all laws rooted in Christian doctrine regarding divorce, homosexuality, abortion—and the purge of all Christian symbols, books, and practices from public schools. It captured and converted not only many of the young, but most of the academy, media, and Hollywood . . . because that is where popularity lay and because they despised the America they had grown up in." Patrick J. Buchanan, *Day of Reckoning: How Hubris, Ideology and Greed Are Tearing America Apart* (New York: St. Martin's Press, 2007), 176–177. In his 1951 book *God and Man at Yale: The Superstitions of Academic Freedom* (Washington DC: Regnery Publishing, 1986), William F. Buckley Jr. argued that "Yale was undermining its students' faith in Christianity." He prescribed to restrict academic freedom such that Christianity and political freedom are always upheld. (Yale was originally a conservative Christian institution but had become more and more secular and liberal.)

5. John Paul II, *Evangelium Vitae,* The Holy See, 1995, http ://w2.vatican.va/content/john-paul-ii/en/encyclicals /documents/hf_jp-ii_enc_25031995_evangelium-vitae.html.

6. Ibid.

7. Ibid.

8. Ibid.

9. Ibid.

10. Ken Ammi, "Atheism," Creation Ministries International, June 18, 2009, http://creation.com /atheism#atheism-communism.

11. Robert Muggah and Renata Giannini, "Interactive Map Tracks Murder Rate Worldwide," IPI Global Observatory, May 19, 2015, https://theglobalobservatory.org/2015/05 /homicide-monitor-brazil-mapping/.

12. "Media Centre: Suicide (Fact Sheet)," World Health Organization, http://www.who.int/mental_health /suicide-prevention/en/.

13. Sabrina Tavernise, "U.S. Suicide Rate Surges to a 30-Year High," *New York Times*, April 22, 2016, https://www.nytimes .com/2016/04/22/health/us-suicide-rate-surges-to-a-30-year -high.html; "Suicide Statistics," American Foundation for Suicide Prevention, https://afsp.org/about-suicide/suicide-statistics/.

14. Gregg Zoroya, "40,000 Suicides Annually, yet America Simply Shrugs," *USA Today*, October 9, 2014, https://www.usatoday .com/story/news/nation/2014/10/09/suicide-mental-health -prevention-research/15276353/.

15. Thomas W. Jacobson and William Robert Johnston, "Abortion Worldwide Report," *The Global Life Campaign*, 2017, https ://www.globallifecampaign.com/abortion-worldwide-report and William Robert Johnston, "Chart Summary of Reported Abortions Worldwide Through August, 2015," http://www .johnstonsarchive.net/policy/abortion/wrjp3314.html.

16. Steven Ertelt, "New Report Claiming 56 Million Abortions Worldwide Every Year Wildly Inflated the Numbers," LifeNews.com, May 26, 2016, http://www.lifenews. com/2016/05/26/new-report-claiming-56-million-abortions -worldwide-every-year-wildly-inflated-the-numbers /. "Abortion Rates Declined Significantly in the Developed World Between 1990 and 2014," Guttmacher Institute, May 11, 2016, https://www.guttmacher.org/news-release/2016 /abortion-rates-declined-significantly-developed-world- between-1990-and-2014.

17. "Number of Abortions—Abortion Counters."

18. According to the Guttmacher Institute: "Approximately 926,200 abortions were performed in 2014, down 12% from 1.06 million in 2011." "Fact Sheet: Induced Abortion in the United States," Guttmacher Institute, October 2017, https://www.guttmacher .org/fact-sheet/induced-abortion-united-states#2.

19. Tara C. Jatlaoui, et al., "Abortion Surveillance–United States, 2013," Morbidity and Mortality Weekly Report, *Surveillance Summaries* 65, no. 12 (2016): 1–44, http://dx.doi.org/10.15585 /mmwr.ss6512a1.

20. C. Mansfield, S. Hopfer, and T. M. Marteau, "Termination Rates After Prenatal Diagnosis of Down's Syndrome, Spina Bifida, Anencephaly, and Turner and Klinefelter Syndromes: A Systematic Literature Review; European Concerted Action: DADA (Decision-Making After the Diagnosis of a Fetal Abnormality)," Prenatal Diagnosis 19, no. 9 (1999): 808–812, https://www.ncbi.nlm.nih.go v/pubmed/10521836. Quoted in Brian G. Skotko, "With New Prenatal Testing, Will Babies with Down's Syndrome Slowly Disappear?," *Archives of Disease in Childhood* 94, no. 11 (2009): 823–826, doi: 10.1136 /adc.2009.166017.

21. Angelina E. Theodorou and Aleksandra Sandstrom, "How Abortion Is Regulated Around the World," Pew Research Center, October 6, 2015, http://www.pewresearch.org /fact-tank/2015/10/06/how-abortion-is-regulated-around -the-world/. According to the Pew Research Center, 58 nations permit abortion "on request"; that is, for any reason at all. In such countries, a mother may terminate her unborn child on the basis of gender and do so openly. If a family wants a boy and tests show that the child in the womb is a girl, an abortion may be performed, no questions asked. Scores more countries allow abortion "to preserve a woman's mental health" or "for economic or social reasons." A mother who seeks—or is coerced into seeking—a sex selection abortion in one of these nations need only couch her reason for the termination in the proper terms for the procedure to be permitted.

22. "China New 'Two-Child' Policy Increases Births by 7.9%, Government Says," CBS News, January 23, 2017, https://www .cbsnews.com/news/china-new-two-child-policy-increases- births-7-percent-government-says/.

23. Mei Fong chronicled a harrowing account of the policy in China in the *New York Post*: "Sterilization, Abortion, Fines: How China Brutally Enforced Its 1-Child Policy," *New York Post*, January 3, 2016, http://nypost.com/2016/01/03/how-chinas-pregnancy-police-brutally-enforced-the-one-child-policy/.

24. Lydia Saad, "In U.S., Nonreligious, Postgrads Are Highly 'Pro-Choice,'" Gallup, May 29, 2012, http://www.gallup.com/poll/154946/non-christians-postgradshighlyprochoice.aspx.

25. Alex Schadenberg, "Euthanasia Rate in Netherlands Has Increased 73% Since 2003," Life News, July 31, 2012, http://www.lifenews.com/2012/07/31/euthanasia-rate-in-netherlands-has-increased-73-since-2003/.

26. Bradford Richardson, "Mark Langedijk, Dutch Man, Euthanized over Alcoholism," *Washington Times*, November 30, 2016, http://www.washingtontimes.com/news/2016/nov/30/mark-langedijk-dutch-man-euthanized-over-alcoholis/.

27. Tragically, in September 2016, the first terminally ill minor was euthanized in Belgium. "The child, who was suffering from an incurable disease, had asked for euthanasia." Chandrika Narayan, "First Child Dies by Euthanasia in Belgium," CNN, September 17, 2016, http://www.cnn.com/2016/09/17/health/belgium-minor-euthanasia/.

28. "Panel Clears Dutch Doctor Who Asked Family Members to Hold Patient Down as She Carried Out Euthanasia Procedure," *Telegraph*, January 28, 2017, http://www.telegraph.co.uk/news/2017/01/28/panel-clears-dutch-doctor-asked-family-hold-patient-carried/.

29. Washington, Oregon, California, Vermont, Colorado, and Montana currently have laws permitting assisted suicide. Angela Chen, "Assisted Suicide Is Now Legal in Colorado," The Verge, November 8, 2016, http://www.theverge.com/2016/11/8/13520908/assisted-suicide-colorado-death-dignity-right-die-election-2016.

30. "I saw it in my sister's case and I see it in the stories from the families who call us. And one of the most pathetic lies out there is that killing someone by denying them food and water is a 'peaceful' and 'painless' experience, and the patently absurd notion that it is a 'death with dignity.'" Bobby Schindler, "I Will Never Forget the Look of Horror on My Sister Terri Schiavo's Face the Day She Died," Life News, March 30, 2015, http ://www.lifenews.com/2015/03/30/i-will-never-forget-the -look-of-horror-on-my-sister-terri-schiavos-face-the -day-she-died/.

31. Susan Donaldson James, "Death Drugs Cause Uproar in Oregon," ABC News, August 6, 2008, http://abcnews.go.com /Health/story?id=5517492.

32. Richard Dawkins, Twitter post, August 20, 2014, https://twitter .com/richarddawkins/status/502106262088466432?lang=en.

33. "Richard Dawkins Apologises for Causing Storm with Down's Syndrome Tweet," *Guardian*, August 21, 2014, https://www .theguardian.com/science/2014/aug/21/richard-dawkins -apologises-downs-syndrome-tweet.

34. J. D. Flynn, "An Open Letter to Richard Dawkins," *First Things*, August 22, 2014, https://www.firstthings.com /web-exclusives/2014/08/an-open-letter-to-richard-dawkins.

35. "Advanced Biosciences Resources (ABR) had a 'technician' embedded at a Planned Parenthood clinic who reportedly harvested and sold the skin of a Down Syndrome baby for $325. Yes, that's correct, in America today, you can buy the skin of an aborted Down Syndrome child for $325. The same baby's leg was sold for $325. . . . The House investigation found one case where Stem Express harvested an intact aborted baby's brain at a Planned Parenthood clinic. They reportedly paid Planned Parenthood $55 but sold the brain to a researcher for over $3000—that's a 2,800% profit. Planned Parenthood reportedly made their money on volume sales and 'charitable donations' from these body harvesting companies." Phelim McAleer,

"McAleer: Congress's Planned Parenthood Investigations Find Horrifying, Criminal Practices," Breitbart, January 15, 2017, http://www.breitbart.com/big-government/2017/01/15/mcaleer-planned-parenthood-investigation-finds-horrifying-criminal-practices/.

36. Thomas D. Williams, "Sierra Club Chief: Abortion Is Key to 'Sustainable Population,'" Breitbart, February 3, 2017, http://www.breitbart.com/big-government/2017/02/03/sierra-club-chief-abortion-key-sustainable-population/.

37. Bre Payton, "A Disabled Lawmaker Speaks Out About Abortion: 'People Like Me' Are Facing Extinction," *Federalist*, January 30, 2017, http://thefederalist.com/2017/01/30/disabled-lawmaker-speak-out-about-abortion-says-people-like-me-face-extinction/.

38. "[Peter] Singer has been a champion of the idea of full moral status being granted only to those things which satisfy the criteria of personhood. . . . Among those who do not qualify for personhood, and thus full moral status, are those with dementia." Stephen W. Smith, *End of Life Decisions in Medical Care: Principles and Policies for Regulating the Dying Process* (Cambridge: Cambridge University Press, 2012), 27. Michael Specter's *New Yorker* profile of Singer demonstrated that when it came to his own mother's battle with dementia, he was willing to spend thousands of dollars to care for her. Michael Specter, "The Dangerous Philosopher," *New Yorker*, September 6, 1999.

39. Margaret Sanger, *Woman and the New Race* (New York: Truth Publishing Company, 1920), 63.

40. Margaret Sanger, "America Needs a Code for Babies," *American Weekly*, March 27, 1934, *NYU.edu*, https://www.nyu.edu/projects/sanger/webedition/app/documents/show.php?sangerDoc=101807.xml.

41. Margaret Sanger, *The Pivot of Civilization* (New York: Brentano's Publishers, 1922), 112.

42. Margaret Sanger, "My Way to Peace," (speech, New History Society, January 17, 1932), NYU.edu, 2003, https://www .nyu.edu/projects/sanger/webedition/app/documents/show .php?sangerDoc=129037.xml.

43. Margaret Sanger, "Letter from Margaret Sanger to Dr. C. J. Gamble, December 10, 1939," Smith College Libraries, https ://libex.smith.edu/omeka/items/show/495.

44. "Bradley Mattes, Executive Director of Life Issues Institute, added: 'This solid evidence is overwhelmingly convincing that Planned Parenthood's business model is to generate income from an increased number of abortions in minority neighborhoods.' . . . 'These census results clearly show that Planned Parenthood continues to pursue the eugenics philosophy of its founder, Margaret Sanger, who believed that Blacks and the poor were 'unfit' to reproduce." Steven Ertelt, "79% of Planned Parenthood Abortion Clinics Target Blacks, Hispanics," Life News, October 16, 2012, http://www.lifenews .com/2012/10/16/79-of-planned-parenthood-abortion-clinics -target-blacks-hispanics/.

45. Conor Beck, "More Black Babies in New York City Are Aborted Than Born Alive," Life News, February 3, 2016, http://www.lifenews.com/2016/02/03/more-black-babies-in -new-york-city-are-aborted-than-born-alive/.

46. Michael W. Chapman, "In Mississippi, 72% of the Babies Aborted Are Black," CNS News, February 25, 2014, http ://www.cnsnews.com/news/article/michael-w-chapman /mississippi-72-babies-aborted-are-black.

47. Udo Schuklenk, "Physicians Can Justifiably Euthanize Certain Severely Impaired Neonates," *Journal of Thoracic and Cardiovascular Surgery* 149, no. 2 (2015): 537.

48. Elizabeth Day, "Infanticide Is Justifiable in Some Cases, Says Ethics Professor," *Telegraph*, January 25, 2004, http ://www.telegraph.co.uk/news/uknews/1452504/Infanticide -is-justifiable-in-some-cases-says-ethics-professor.html.

49. Alberto Giubilini and Francesca Minerva, "After Birth Abortion: Why Should the Baby Live?," *Journal of Medical Ethics* 39, no. 5 (2013), accessed November 6, 2017, doi: http://jme .bmj.com/content/39/5/261.

Chapter 8: The Faithfulness of the Atheists

1. This epigram is universally attributed to G. K. Chesterton, though its exact source is difficult to locate. It is in *The Wit and Wisdom of the 20th Century: A Book of Quotations* (New York: Peter Bedrick, 1987) and has been associated with a quote from page 211 of Émile Cammaerts's book *The Laughing Prophet: The Seven Virtues and G. K. Chesterton* (London: Methuen, 1937).

2. "In Lucretius' *The Nature of the Universe*—which is the greatest classical statement of a system of atheism—it is argued that it is impossible that matter was created and that it must, therefore, be eternal and uncreated. The basis of this argument is the general causal principle: 'Nothing can come from nothing.' . . . Hume develops an account of causation that directly contradicts these causal principles. Contrary to the causal maxim, Hume maintains, it is entirely possible for us to conceive of something beginning to exist without any cause." Paul Russel and Anders Kraal, *The Stanford Encyclopedia of Philosophy*, October 4, 2005, https://plato.stanford.edu/entries/ hume-religion/.

3. "Kepler's first law of planetary motion states that the orbit of every planet is an ellipse [a squashed circle] with the Sun at its focus." Timothy Kusky, "Kepler, Johannes," *Encyclopedia of Earth and Space Science*, ed. Katherine E. Cullen (New York: Facts on File, 2010), 483. "The Sun–in fact our whole solar system– orbits around the center of the Milky Way Galaxy." "StarChild Question of the Month for February 2000," StarChild, February 2000, https://starchild.gsfc.nasa.gov/docs/StarChild/questions /question18.html.

4. "Astronomers have been able to determine that there is a

hierarchical organization to the universe, with matter organized into progressively larger structures from atoms, to solar systems, to galaxies, to clusters and superclusters, to filaments, then a continued structure known as the End of Greatness." Timothy Kusky, *Encyclopedia of Earth and Space Science*, ed. Katherine E. Cullen (New York: Facts on File, 2010), 789.

5. "The probability of constructing a rather short functional protein at random becomes so small as to be effectively zero (1 chance in 10125) even given our multibillion-year-old universe." Stephen C. Meyer, "The Explanatory Power of Design," in *Mere Creation: Science, Faith and Intelligent Design*, ed. William A. Dembski (Downers Grove, IL: InterVarsity Press, 1998), 126.

6. Michael J. Behe, William A. Dembski, and Stephen C. Meyer, *Science and Evidence for Design in the Universe* (San Francisco: Ignatius Press, 2000), 93.

7. C. S. Lewis, *Mere Christianity* (New York: HarperOne, 2001), 35.

8. Kusky, *Encyclopedia of Earth and Space Science*, 191.

9. "It seems as though we must use sometimes the one theory and sometimes the other, while at times we may use either. We are faced with a new kind of difficulty. We have two contradictory pictures of reality; separately neither of them fully explains the phenomena of light, but together they do." Albert Einstein and Leopold Infeld, *The Evolution of Physics* (New York: Touchstone, 1967), 262–63.

10. Adam Becker, "Why Does Time Always Run Forwards and Never Backwards?" BBC, March 9, 2015, http://www.bbc .com/earth/story/20150309-why-does-time-only-run-forwards.

11. "Our physical spacetime is four-dimensional, with one time dimension and three space dimensions. . . . In string theory, on the other hand, the number of spacetime dimensions emerges from a calculation. The answer is not four, but rather ten." Barton Zwiebach, *A First Course in String Theory*, 2nd ed. (Cambridge: Cambridge University Press, 2009), 7.

12. "Relativity and quantum mechanics are fundamentally different theories that have different formulations. It is not just a matter of scientific terminology; it is a clash of genuinely incompatible descriptions of reality. The conflict between the two halves of physics has been brewing for more than a century—sparked by a pair of 1905 papers by Einstein, one outlining relativity and the other introducing the quantum." Corey S. Powell, "Will Quantum Mechanics Swallow Relativity?" *Nautilus*, October 29, 2015, http://nautil.us/issue/29/scaling/will-quantum-mechanics-swallow-relativity.

13. Clara Moskowitz, assistant managing editor of Space.com, delves into the contradictions of black holes, general relativity, and quantum mechanics in her article "Black Holes: Everything You Think You Know Is Wrong," Space.com, August 2, 2012, https://www.space.com/16867-black-holes-quantum-mechanics-theory.html.

14. This is self-contradictory, as gravity is a part of nature and nature could not cause itself to come into being.

15. "The very nature of the scientific enterprise is at stake in the multiverse debate. Its advocates propose weakening the nature of scientific proof in order to claim that the multiverse hypothesis provides a scientific explanation. This is a dangerous tactic. Two central scientific virtues are testability and explanatory power. In the cosmological context, these are often in conflict with each other and there has been an increasing tendency in theoretical physics and cosmology to say it does not matter whether a proposal is testable: if it fits into our other theories in a convincing way, with great explanatory power, then testing is superfluous. The extreme case is the multiverse proposal, where no direct observational test of the hypothesis is possible. Despite this, many articles and books dogmatically proclaim that the multiverse is an established scientific fact." George Ellis, "Opposing the Multiverse," *A&G* 49, no. 2 (2008): 2.33–2.35.

16. Mortimer J. Adler, *How to Prove There Is a God: Mortimer J.*

Adler's Writings and Thoughts About God, ed. Ken Dzugan (Chicago: Open Court, 2011), 10.

17. Dawkins made this comment when accepting the Humanist of the Year Award from the American Humanist Association in 1996. Quoted in Alex Berezow, "Richard Dawkins Is Wrong About Religion," *Forbes,* September 30, 2013, https://www .forbes.com/sites/alexberezow/2013/09/30 /richard-dawkins-is-wrong-about-religion/#24958c9319ef.

18. Reza Aslan, quoted in Chris Stedman, "'Evangelical Atheists:' Pushing for What?" *Huffington Post*, October 18, 2010, http ://www.huffingtonpost.com/chris-stedman/evangelical -atheists-what_b_765379.html.

Chapter 9: The Malevolence of the Atheists

1. Gabe Bullard, "The World's Newest Major Religion: No Religion," *National Geographic*, April 22, 2016, http://news. nationalgeographic.com/2016/04/160422-atheism-agnostic -secular-nones-rising-religion/.

2. Carolyn Gregoire, "Happiness Index: Only 1 In 3 Americans Are Very Happy, According to Harris Poll," *Huffington Post*, June 1, 2013, http://www.huffingtonpost.com/2013/06/01 /happiness-indexonly1in_n_3354524.html.

3. Marina Marcus et al., "Depression: A Global Public Health Concern," World Health Organization, 2012, http://www .who.int/mental_health/management/depression/who_paper _depression_wfmh_2012.pdf.

4. Lee Habeeb on the media's secularization of Martin Luther King Jr.: "You'll hear endless references to Dr. Martin Luther King this week—but never to Reverend King. The clips you'll hear, the videos you'll see, will be King's stirring secular rhetoric. What you will not hear are the parts of the speeches filled with references to God. Or the book from which sprang the source of this man's devotion to justice: the Bible." Lee Habeeb, "The Secularization of Martin Luther King Jr." LifeZette, January 15,

2017, http://www.lifezette.com/popzette/secularization-martin
-luther-king-jr/.

5. G. K. Chesterton, quoted in Francis S. Collins, *The Language of God: A Scientist Presents Evidence for Belief* (New York: Free Press, 2006), 300.

6. Ravi Zacharias, *The Real Face of Atheism* (Grand Rapids: Baker Books, 2009), 98, 101.

7. John Stossel and Kristina Kendall, "Who Gives and Who Doesn't," ABC News, November 28, 2006, http://abcnews .go.com/2020/Story?id=2682730&page=2. Further, a study conducted by Barna in 2007 found: "The typical no-faith American donated just $200 in 2006, which is more than seven times less than the amount contributed by the prototypical active-faith adult ($1500). Even when church-based giving is subtracted from the equation, active-faith adults donated twice as many dollars last year as did atheists and agnostics." "Atheists and Agnostics Take Aim at Christians," Barna, June 11, 2007, https://www.barna.com/research/atheists-and-agnostics-take -aim-at-christians/.

8. John 11:25–26 NIV.

9. Charles Dickens, *A Christmas Carol* (London: Bradbury & Evans, 1858), 5.

10. Terry Eagleton, Harvard literature professor and well-known critic of new atheism, notes how foolish Richard Dawkins looks in light of God as Creator: "There is thus a curious connection between the doctrine of creation out of nothing and the professional life of Richard Dawkins. Without God, Dawkins would be out of a job. It is thus particularly churlish of him to call the existence of his employer into question." Terry Eagleton, *Reason, Faith, and Revolution: Reflections on the God Debate* (New Haven: Yale University Press, 2009), 9.

11. Genesis 1:26.

12. Numerous passages in Scripture refer to the Devil, the fallen angels, and their war against the angels of God: "Then war

broke out in heaven. Michael and his angels fought against the dragon, and the dragon and his angels fought back. But he was not strong enough, and they lost their place in heaven. The great dragon was hurled down—that ancient serpent called the devil, or Satan, who leads the whole world astray. He was hurled to the earth, and his angels with him" (Revelation 12:7–9 NIV); "The angels who did not keep their positions of authority but abandoned their proper dwelling—these he has kept in darkness, bound with everlasting chains for judgment on the great Day" (Jude v. 6 NIV). See also Isaiah 14:12–15; Ezekiel 28:12–15; Luke 10:18; John 8:44; and Revelation 12:4.

13. Matthew 26:53: "Do you think that I cannot appeal to my Father, and he will at once send me more than twelve legions of angels?" Luke 2:13: "And suddenly there was with the angel a multitude of the heavenly host praising God."

14. Luke 22:19. See also 1 Corinthians 11:24.

15. Frank Pavone, "This Is My Body," Priests for Life, April 29, 1997, http://www.priestsforlife.org /library/217-this-is-my-body.

Chapter 10: The End of the Atheists

1. Hitchens continued to participate in debates with religious proponents during his illness, making public appearances until two months before his death on December 15, 2011. In his October 2010 column in *Vanity Fair*, he responded graciously to well-wishers and expressed contempt for ill-wishers. He talked about his cancer and atheism in an August 2010 interview on *ABC Lateline* with Tony Jones and with Brian Lamb on CSPAN's *Q&A*. Christopher Hitchens, "Unanswerable Prayers," *Vanity Fair*, September 2010, http://www.vanityfair.com /culture/2010/10/hitchens-201010.

2. Deuteronomy 6:16. See also Matthew 4:7 and Luke 4:12.

3. Tony Jones, "Hitchens' Last Days: Carol Blue, Christopher Hitchens' Widow, Talks Candidly About her Husband's Dying

Days," *ABC Lateline*, October 26, 2012, http://www.abc.net.au /lateline/content/2012/s3619164.htm.

    A portion of the transcript of Tony Jones's interview with Hitchens's widow, Carol Blue, on ABC's *Lateline:*

    TONY JONES: "Here's a strange thing that I discovered reading the book, Carol. In this weakened and vulnerable state, the great atheist finds himself confined to bed unable to avoid the sight on the wall of a large black crucifix, as he said, embedded into the wall in his hospital room. This must have been some kind of torture for him as well."

    CAROL BLUE: "Yeah, he thought it was odd because we were in a hospital—he was in a hospital in Washington—Georgetown Hospital, which is a Catholic hospital, and there was a huge cross on top of every door, so it was a little unsettling because you think, 'Mmm, perhaps we'd like to see a picture of the human genome. Perhaps that would be preferable to a giant cross. I mean, how far is this gonna get you in the modern world of medicine?' But it didn't bother him. And in fact he always liked talking to the various chaplains and assorted religious figures that seemed to haunt the halls of hospitals. He was always willing to have a long babble with them."

    TONY JONES: "Debating right to the end on the nature of belief."

    CAROL BLUE: "Yes."

4. Hitchens received treatment for his cancer at the Georgetown Lombardi Comprehensive Cancer Center, part of Georgetown University Medical Center—a Jesuit institution—but died at the University of Texas MD Anderson Cancer in Houston, Texas, on December 15, 2011.

5. Andrew Sullivan, "The Hitch Has Landed," *The Dish* (blog), April 20, 2012, http://dish.andrewsullivan.com/2012/04/20 /hitchs-service/. Andrew Sullivan wrote about Hitchens's final moments as witnessed by Steve Wasserman and others: "And

then his last words. As he lay dying, he asked for a pen and paper and tried to write on it. After a while, he finished, held it up, looked at it, and saw that it was an illegible assemblage of scribbled, meaningless hieroglyphics. 'What's the use?' he said to Steve Wasserman. Then he dozed a little and then roused himself and uttered a couple of words that were close to inaudible. Steve asked him to repeat them. There were two: 'Capitalism.' 'Downfall.'"

6. Flew was awarded the In Praise of Reason Award in 1985, the highest honor the Committee for Skeptical Inquiry awards. It was presented by CSICOP chairman Paul Kurtz in London. "'In Praise of Reason' Award Goes to Antony Flew," *Skeptical Inquirer* 10, no. 2 (1985): 102, 104; "NZARH Honorary Associates," New Zealand Association of Rationalists and Humanists, http ://rationalists.nz/about/associates.

7. "The only conclusion I can draw is that these apologists are taking advantage of a confused, elderly man in a state of cognitive decline. There's little evidence that Flew even understands the controversy he's at the center of, much less that he changed his position as the result of any new arguments." Adam Lee, "The Exploitation of Antony Flew," *Daylight Atheism* (blog), Patheos, November 6, 2007, http://www.patheos.com /blogs/daylightatheism/2007/11/the-exploitation-of-antony -flew. Lee blindly accepted the finding of Mark Oppenheimer in his November 4, 2007, *New York Times* interview that Flew's "mental powers [were] in decline." This was three years after Flew's 2004 conversion, the year assessing his "mental powers" may have been reasonable. Funny how the atheists had forgotten that in December 2004, Flew, with his characteristic alacrity and erudition, spelled out his newfound belief in an exclusive interview with Professor Gary Habermas ("My Pilgrimage from Atheism to Theism: An Exclusive Interview with Former British Atheist Professor Antony Flew," *Philosophia Christi* 6, no. 2, 2004. *Philosophia Christi* is a journal published by Biola).

Contrary to the wishful thinking of Mark Oppenheimer and Adam Lee, Flew was well aware of, in the words of Lee, the "controversy he was at the center of."

8. Antony Flew, "Exclusive Flew Interview," interview by Benjamin Wiker, To The Source, October 30, 2007, http ://tothesource.org/2007/10/.

9. John 7:38; John 4:14; John 4:10.

10. "The Future of World Religions: Population Growth Projections, 2010–2050," Pew Research Center, April 2, 2015, http://www.pewforum.org/2015/04/02/religious-projections -2010-2050/.

11. Ibid.

12. Ibid.

13. Conrad Hackett and Brian J. Grim, "Global Christianity: A Report on the Size and Distribution of the World's Christian Population," Pew Research Center: The Pew Forum on Religion and Public Life, December 2011, http://www .pewforum.org/files/2011/12/Christianity-fullreport-web.pdf.

14. Ibid.

15. Ibid.

16. Rodney Stark and Xiuhua Wang, *A Star in the East: The Rise of Christianity in China* (West Conshohocken, PA: Templeton Press, 2015), 90.

17. "The Future of World Religions: Population Growth Projections, 2010–2050," Pew Research Center, April 2, 2015, http://www.pewforum.org/2015/04/02/religious-projections -2010–2050/.

18. This is a variation of Anthony DeStefano's treatment of the agnostic position in his book *Angels All Around Us: A Sightseeing Guide to the Invisible World* (New York: Image, 2012). See chapter 10, "Seeing the Invisible," page 200.

19. G. K. Chesterton, *The Everlasting Man* (New York: Dover Publications, 2012), 244.

20. Matthew 24:35 NIV.